Differentiated Instruction for the Middle School Math Teacher

Jossey-Bass Teacher provides K–12 teachers with essential knowledge and tools to create a positive and lifelong impact on student learning. Trusted and experienced educational mentors offer practical classroom-tested and theory-based teaching resources for improving teaching practice in a broad range of grade levels and subject areas. From one educator to another, we want to be your first source to make every day your best day in teaching. *Jossey-Bass Teacher* resources serve two types of informational needs—essential knowledge and essential tools.

Essential knowledge resources provide the foundation, strategies, and methods from which teachers may design curriculum and instruction to challenge and excite their students. Connecting theory to practice, essential knowledge books rely on a solid research base and time-tested methods, offering the best ideas and guidance from many of the most experienced and well-respected experts in the field.

Essential tools save teachers time and effort by offering proven, ready-to-use materials for in-class use. Our publications include activities, assessments, exercises, instruments, games, ready reference, and more. They enhance an entire course of study, a weekly lesson, or a daily plan. These essential tools provide insightful, practical, and comprehensive materials on topics that matter most to K–12 teachers.

JB JOSSEY-BASS

Differentiated Instruction for the Middle School Math Teacher

Activities and Strategies for an Inclusive Classroom

Joan D'Amico and Kate Gallaway

Foreword by Gloria Sanok

BICENTENNIAL
1807
WILEY
2007
BICENTENNIAL

John Wiley & Sons, Inc.

Published by Jossey-Bass
A Wiley Imprint
989 Market Street, San Francisco, CA 94103-1741   www.josseybass.com

Illustrations by Alice Beresin.

Wiley Bicentennial logo: Richard J. Pacifico

Jossey-Bass books and products are available through most bookstores. To contact Jossey-Bass directly call our Customer Care Department within the U.S. at 800-956-7739, outside the U.S. at 317-572-3986, or fax 317-572-4002.

Jossey-Bass also publishes its books in a variety of electronic formats. Some content that appears in print may not be available in electronic books.

Library of Congress Cataloging-in-Publication Data

D'Amico, Joan, date–
  Differentiated instruction for the middle school math teacher: activities and strategies for an inclusive classroom / Joan D'Amico and Kate Gallaway.
      p. cm.
  Includes bibliographical references.
  ISBN 978-0-7879-8468-7 (alk. paper)
  1. Mathematics—Study and teaching (Middle school)—Activity programs. 2. Middle school teaching.
I. Gallaway, Kate. II. Title.
  QA11.2.D327 2007
  510.71'2—dc22
                                                                        2007031401

Printed in the United States of America
FIRST EDITION
PB Printing   10 9 8 7 6 5 4 3 2 1

Contents

About This Book

The goal of this book is to help middle school math teachers effectively teach the wide range of students in their classrooms. The middle school mathematics classroom is a unique learning environment. The cognitive load is high as the mathematical content becomes more complex, requiring students to remember facts and formulas while at the same time using them to solve problems. Teaching a class filled with students of varying learning styles and skill levels can be tricky.

This book is a practical, easy-to-use answer to this environment. It shows you effective ways to present mathematical concepts to the whole class and how to provide opportunities for guided practice, as well as to modify the material to provide access to the same content standard for all students. Just as important, it shows how to involve the students' families and tie each math concept to their everyday lives. Relevance is a powerful motivator. The conversational style and thoroughness of this book, as well as the reproducible worksheets and activities, make it easy to start using right away.

Here's what you will find in this book.

Part One provides an overview of general techniques for being successful in an inclusive classroom environment. Chapter One focuses on successful collaboration with the school team, as well as parents and families. Several checklists help streamline this process. Chapter Two explores assessing learning style to differentiate instruction. There are several ways to assess students so that you can choose the method that works best for you. Chapter Three offers tips for successful instruction in the inclusive classroom, including alternative assessment techniques.

Part Two is where you'll find specific activities. The activities in these chapters conform to the NCTM content standards, making it efficient to integrate them into your instruction. They are designed to help you differentiate instruction for your inclusive classroom. At the beginning of each activity is a statement of its purpose and a list of supplies you will need. Then each activity walks you through presenting a lesson to the whole class. This is followed by a worksheet designed for review and reinforcement of the concepts presented in the lesson. Students may complete the worksheet as is, or you may use it as a pretest to identify the levels of your students' understanding. Each activity includes a section entitled "How to Adapt This Lesson for the Inclusive Classroom," which offers a variety of teaching strategies, methods, and tools to use in appropriate stations to differentiate instruction. These stations provide a multitude of modalities offered to remediate, reinforce, or enrich the concept presented. Another section, "Home/School Connection," can be used to invite parents to be part of the learning process. Activities here are family based and include life skills and practical learning. At the end of each activity are suggestions for assessing how well the students have learned the concepts and skills presented.

The Glossary at the end of the book covers the terms used throughout the lessons, and the Bibliography lists additional resources.

You can use these activities as an integral component of your math curriculum or as a supplement to the textbook, and you can adapt the format to your individual curriculum needs.

About the Authors

Joan D'Amico, M.A., is a learning disabilities teacher/consultant in the Garfield School District in New Jersey and has a private practice as a learning disabilities specialist. While teaching middle school for seven years in Wayne, New Jersey, she won the New Jersey Governor's Teaching for Excellence Award. In addition, she has taught workshops in elementary and middle schools, as well as conducted seminars in the business sector for teachers and students teaching academic concepts using multisensory activities. She has appeared on CNN, TNN, and the Food Network. D'Amico is a member of the New Jersey Association of Learning Consultants and the American Federation of Teachers (AFT).

She is also a coauthor of a series of seven books published by John Wiley & Sons that focuses on teaching academic subjects using food and cooking, creative experiments, and multisensory activities. Among them are *The Science Chef, The Math Chef, The Healthy Body Cookbook,* and *The Coming to America Cookbook.*

Kate Gallaway, M.A., is a professor at Chapman University in Monterey, California, and frequently makes public appearances across the country at conferences and to different parent groups. She also has a private practice in Carmel, California, specializing in math and study skills, and she has worked with children of all ages. She is an educational therapist with a B.A. in psychology from UCLA and a master's in mild to moderate learning disabilities from San Francisco State University, where she also earned her educational therapist certification. She is a credentialed teacher and the coauthor of the book *Managing the Mathematics Classroom.*

*Dedicated to the art of teaching and to the premise that effective
teaching is the gift of inspiring, motivating, and communicating information
and emotions to all types of learners, allowing them the opportunity to
understand, implement change, and grow*

Acknowledgments

We wish to thank the following individuals:

- Our parents, Joseph and Carol Lange, and Mary and Richard Lind, for being a lifelong source of inspiration and motivation

- Our children, Christi, Alexa, and Kyle D'Amico, and Grant and Pierce Gallaway who challenge us to continually learn and grow

- Husband Ralph D'Amico, for his intellect, eternal fountain of knowledge, and support

- Husband Wally Gallaway, for his confidence in me and unwavering support.

- Our editor, Kate Bradford, for believing in this project from the beginning

- Friend Anthony Rufo, for his constant encouragement and endless hours of script reading

- Friends and colleagues Anne Gunar and Melissa Timochko for being great listeners throughout the project

- Charles Corey, Christi D'Amico and Alexa D'Amico for assisting with the key and preliminary artwork sketches

- Dr. Gloria Sanok, for her wisdom, math expertise and script review

- The wonderful colleagues and friends at Thomas Jefferson Middle School, Garfield Child Study Team, (Garfield, NJ) and Schuyler Colfax Middle School (Wayne, NJ) who generously gave input and ideas when needed

- The students and their families who served as inspiration through their hard work and commitment to learning. You have greatly touched our lives.

Foreword

The experiences I have had in my vast and varied career has made me realize that certain chronological years are critical to school success and development. In the area of mathematics, the middle school grades are of utmost importance, as the young child grows into a teenage student and develops the ability to think logically. It is at this milestone that students begin to formulate more sophisticated ideas and abstract thoughts.

This book, *Differentiated Instruction for the Middle School Math Teacher: Activities and Strategies for an Inclusive Classroom*, by Joan D'Amico and Kate Gallaway, provides a wonderful tool for addressing the needs of all students in the same classroom, thus giving all students the chance to develop and excel in math. The book is written so that teachers can include all students in the learning process, welcoming learning strengths, weaknesses, and individual differences.

The most important part of this book is that it supports a philosophy of providing a variety of instructional techniques and learning modalities so that one classroom can offer all students an appropriate mathematics education for most levels. The activities in this book are so that a lesson is presented to the whole class, then followed by a worksheet designed to reinforce and review the material. Students can also complete the worksheet in stations or small groups, where the instruction is differentiated; various modalities to reinforce the worksheet concepts are presented and tailored to several skill levels.

The modifications presented in this book provide teachers with effective tools to adapt the lessons further. Adaptations for students with learning disabilities, attention deficit–hyperactivity disorder or behavioral concerns, physical disabilities, and gifted students are provided at the end of each activity, giving teachers a wealth of teaching strategies and techniques tailored to specific populations. All of the lessons are fun, quick to set up, easy to use, and use few supplies.

The Home/School Connection section at the end of each activity is designed to build a bridge between the home and school and shows how the lesson can be used in a real-world situation. Each one offers creative and practical activities for students to bring home and complete with their family.

The checklists in Part One aid teachers in collaborating with the Child Study Team, assessing learning styles, and adapting instruction. The chapters in this part present background information on various learning disabilities, learning strengths and weaknesses, multiple intelligences, and learning styles and provide a valuable reference for the teacher's desk.

In the inclusive classroom, teachers must be able to create a flexible environment that is constantly changing to meet the needs of individuals and the group. This book is a valuable resource to aid teachers in developing this flexibility and using strategies, activities, adaptations, and techniques to communicate math to all students while making the subject interesting, practical, and fun.

Gloria Sanok, Ph.D.
Program Developer and Math Education Consultant,
Wayne Schools, New Jersey Gifted and Talented Program

Differentiated Instruction for the Middle School Math Teacher

Part One

Being Successful in the Inclusive Classroom

Chapter 1

Collaborating Effectively

Success in the inclusive classroom is due in large part to collaboration with others in the school. Teaching an inclusive classroom is difficult to do alone, and there are systems in place so that you don't have to. In this chapter, we look at some general ways of making collaboration work for you.

Collaborating for Intervention

All teachers are eager to communicate information to all of their students. If a student is struggling with classroom performance or cannot understand the material presented in class, then you need to assist and monitor this student to try to help him or her. This chapter focuses on what to do when this approach fails: how to help students when the work continues to be difficult even after extra assistance has taken place and there has to be an intervention.

Often a teacher will ask, "What do I do with a student who is having difficulties learning in my class? How can I get him or her help? Do I need to request an evaluation to see if special education is necessary?"

Teachers often bring this topic of discussion to a member of the Child Study Team, for advice. A Child Study Team is a group of specialists who are trained to determine if a child has a learning disability. The team is primarily made up of a psychologist, a learning specialist, and a social worker. The first question that the Child Study Team should pose is, "What prereferral intervention strategies have been implemented, and what was the student outcome?"

Prereferral intervention strategies are generally determined by a committee of general education teachers before any specialists are included in the plan. The committee's job is to try to assist students who are failing subjects within the confines of the general education setting. The student's main subject teachers, along with the guidance counselor, meet to discuss what can be changed in the classroom setting to enhance student progress. Typical prereferral intervention strategies at the middle school level can include these:

- Changing a student's seat
- Calling parents for a conference
- Talking with the student
- Assigning the student to a "study buddy"
- Changing a student's teacher
- Placing the student on a weekly behavioral progress sheet, signed by parents and teachers
- Placing the student on a weekly homework modification sheet to be signed by parents and teachers
- Suggesting after-school assistance or tutoring
- Deciding if the student should attend basic skills classes
- Retention

The teachers then agree to implement specific modifications, as well as decide on a meeting date to monitor the child's progress and determine if the outcome was positive. If progress is not being made, a referral to the Child Study Team may be warranted.

A checklist can be a helpful aid in determining a clear plan of action. This information can be stored in the student's permanent record folder. (See page 5.)

Collaborating with the Child Study Team

Establishing positive relationships with all members of the school is important. In an inclusive classroom, open lines of communication between the general and special education teachers, as well as support personnel, are essential for a thorough understanding of all students' learning needs. Discussions with past and present teachers, as well as a complete record review, can give the middle school teacher insight into planning for students in the inclusive classroom. The Child Study Team can be an excellent resource for further information on a particular student's special needs. The members of the team can also offer assistance in implementing modifications and learning strategies set forth by an Individual Education Program (IEP). An IEP is a document that explains a plan of action and program tailored to a student's specific learning and behavioral needs. This is a legal document. It's contents must be agreed on by the child's parents or guardians and implemented in school by the teachers.

Checklist for Prereferral Interventions

Student name: _____ Date: _____

Reason for meeting: _____

_____

_____

Fill in the following prereferral interventions to be implemented and monitored:

Intervention	Person Responsible	Date Implemented
Calls to parents		
Changing student's seat in the classroom		
Interview with student		
Student to visit guidance counselor		
Parent conference		
Suggestions for after-school assistance or tutoring		
Assigning a study buddy		
Assigning a weekly behavioral progress sheet, signed by parents and teachers		
Recommendation for basic skills or compensatory assistance		
Retention		
Additional classroom interventions		

Comments: _____

_____

_____

_____

Follow-up meeting date: _____

Members of the Child Study Team

The core specialists on the Child Study Team are a psychologist and/or educational therapist and a social worker. (A speech and language specialist is also part of the core team, but only for preschool students.) These individuals are trained in the diagnosis and remediation of learning disabilities. The team may also include additional professionals and paraprofessionals who can offer classroom strategies and home suggestions, such as special and general education teachers, school nurses and other staff, speech and motor therapists, paraprofessionals, and the child's parents.

School Psychologist

In many states, the school psychologist is the main support person responsible for assessing the learning levels of students who are referred to the Child Study Team. They can do this through standardized and nonstandardized assessments that measure learning strengths and weaknesses. The most popular tool used by the school psychologist is an individual IQ (Intelligence Quotient) test. The IQ test, an accepted measure of intellectual functioning nationwide, offers one way to assess students' verbal and nonverbal abilities. The assessment is administered individually and is completed in approximately one two-hour session.

The school psychologist may also assess the student's academic levels in mathematics, reading, written language, and oral language, as well as learning styles and strengths and weaknesses, through specific diagnostic standardized testing instruments, functional assessments, report card grades, teacher interviews, classroom observations, and past standardized test performance.

Finally, the school psychologist assesses any emotional and behavioral concerns that may impede the learning process. This evaluation can be accomplished through interviews with the student, teachers, and parents, as well as through scales and instruments designed to measure these adaptive functions.

The Learning Disabilities Teacher/Consultant or Educational Therapist (LDT/C or Educational Diagnostician)

Not all states have an LDT/C or educational therapist as part of their school team. The main roles of this person as a team member are to complete psychoeducational testing to determine the student's academic strengths and weaknesses and develop remedial modifications to aid in therapeutically teaching the student with disabilities. The LDT/C can also do what a psychologist does as part of the Child Study Team. He or she measures specific levels in mathematics, reading, and written and oral language and then develops skills and strategies to be used in the classroom for remediation.

School Social Worker

The school social worker is responsible for obtaining student and family background information and determining if the child's home life now or in the past is having an impact on his or her educational performance. Family, birth, and developmental history are obtained through an interview with the parents. School social workers also can help students during times of impending or actual individual or school crisis.

Speech and Language Therapists

The job of the speech and language therapist on the Child Study Team is to determine if a student's articulation and language abilities are standing in the way of the child's learning success in school. Through standardized and functional assessment tools, these therapists can determine if the child has weaknesses in phonology, syntax, articulation, and oral and written language. If they diagnose a communication disorder, the Child Study Team can prescribe individual, group, or collaborative therapy.

Special Education Teachers

Special education teachers are trained to teach skills and strategies for remediation purposes and are in part responsible for implementing the educational modifications designated in IEPs. They are knowledgeable in working with students with learning disabilities and can be essential as support teachers, along with paraprofessionals, in the inclusion classroom.

General Education Teachers

General education teachers in the middle school environment are teachers who specialize in one area of the curriculum, such as English, history, math, reading, or science. They collaborate with special education teachers and paraprofessionals to communicate their subject matter effectively to all students in an inclusive classroom. This is accomplished by cooperative planning and development of pretests, worksheets, learning strategies, study guides, modifications, and reviews.

School Nurse

The school nurse is required to complete vision and hearing screenings and check attendance, as well as offer specific nursing services to special and general education students. These services can include administering medications, changing catheters, checking hearing devices, storing wheelchairs, and monitoring blood pressure and sugar levels.

Guidance Counselors

Guidance counselors work as a liaison with the teachers, students, parents, administration, and school team. They arrange prereferral meetings with the teachers to identify and determine intervention strategies for students who are struggling in the general education environment. They also make sure that prereferral interventions are executed and outcomes are monitored. Guidance counselors are responsible for administering standardized tests, recording grades, and monitoring all students. In a middle school environment, it is not unusual to have a guidance counselor assigned to each grade level.

School Administration

Principals, vice principals, and deans of students are part of the school administration. An ongoing relationship between classroom teachers and the school administration is essential when identifying students with learning disabilities or emotional and behavioral difficulties, as these professionals are often the first people to address consequences stemming from the manifestations of student problems in the classroom. The principals and student deans are usually responsible for assigning detentions, suspensions, and expulsions from school.

Physical Therapists

Physical therapists evaluate and provide therapies to strengthen gross motor skills. They provide these services in an individual, small group, or natural setting according to the recommendations of the physical therapist and Child Study Team. Recently there has been an increase in administering therapies in a natural setting, for example, school hallways. For a student who needs strength walking in a natural setting, the therapist walks with the student during passing time. A natural setting does not change or contrive the environment for therapy.

Occupational Therapists

Occupational therapists evaluate and provide therapies to strengthen fine motor and organizational skills. In a younger child, individual therapy often seeks to strengthen hand and finger muscles, correct pencil grip, and help the child gain motor control while writing. For older students, occupational therapists are brought in to help enhance students' written expression and organizational skills. These services are provided in an individual, small group, or natural setting.

Paraprofessionals

Paraprofessionals, part of the school team in an inclusion classroom, assist the teacher in implementing both group and individual lesson plans. They collaborate with the teacher on strategies and ideas, mark papers, teach small group lessons, reinforce and review information presented in class, and arrange materials for small station instruction. They also perform many routine classroom duties such as collecting and organizing class assignments, homework, and projects.

Personal Aides

Personal aides can be part of a special education student's IEP. The personal aide's role is to assist an assigned student with specific personal needs related to the school environment, such as students who may need additional assistance navigating a building with a wheelchair or with a walker, or using an elevator. The checklist on page 9 will help teachers determine whom to confer with first.

Referral Interventions

Sometimes teachers can have great success with minimal modifications within the general education classroom setting. At other times, the learning or behavioral difficulties are too severe, and students continue to do poorly in spite of prereferral intervention strategies. If this is determined, a follow-up meeting may be scheduled to discuss the possibilities of a referral to the Child Study Team. If possible Child Study Team services have been decided at this meeting, a referral form is then filled out by one or more teachers to be addressed by the Intervention and Referral Services Committee (IRS).

The IRS includes at least one general and one special education teacher, the guidance counselor, and one member of the Child Study Team. The referring teacher brings information on current classroom performance, grades, and results of the prereferral intervention strategies that were implemented for the child in question. The committee, with the help of the Child Study Team representative, decides if a team evaluation is warranted at this time.

Prereferral Collaboration with School Personnel Checklist

Teachers who encounter problem situations do not always know whom to ask for assistance or advice. Complete the following exercise to test your own knowledge of personnel roles and resources.

Whom Should I Confer with First?

Use the information that has been presented so far in this chapter and advice from your own Child Study Team to determine the best person to speak to first regarding initial concerns about a student. Read through the following situations and use the list of abbreviations at the end of the list to mark each concern with the appropriate person to talk to.

_____ Andrew may need to go to summer school, or retaining him or her seems evident.

_____ Joshua has difficulties completing math homework, and his grade average for the marking period will be lower as a result.

_____ In spite of several intervention strategies, Tyler has difficulties with reading comprehension skills.

_____ Eric sits in the back of the classroom all day and doesn't make eye contact with anyone. He is not completing his work.

_____ Brianna broke her leg and needs a key to the elevator.

_____ Aisha has severe headaches and needs medication at lunchtime in school.

_____ Sarah was caught cheating during a midterm exam.

_____ Elle, a new student with spina bifida needs additional exercises added to his program.

_____ Part of a new program is to set up station materials for students to learn math in different modalities.

_____ Alex needs a study guide for an upcoming social studies test.

_____ Michael's handwriting looks very labored and resembles that of a much younger child.

_____ Several students were upset after the unexpected death of a classmate.

_____ Last year in sixth grade, Juan did well in science, but this year he is failing the class.

List of Abbreviations

Psy = School psychologist	Para = Paraprofessional
LDT/C = Learning consultant or educational therapist	Gui = Guidance
Soc = School social worker	Adm = Administration
OT = Occupational therapist	Spec = Special education teacher
PT = Physical therapist	Gen = General education teacher

The Case Manager

If the IRS committee decides that a Child Study Team evaluation might be warranted, a person on the team who is designated to be the case manager contacts the parents. Throughout the evaluation process, the case manager has these responsibilities:

- Facilitating communication between the parents and the school staff
- Communicating with the guidance counselor and teachers
- Understanding the student's learning strengths and weaknesses in the classroom
- Becoming knowledgeable of the student's abilities, home circumstances, and ongoing progress in school throughout the evaluation
- Understanding and implementing time lines for prompt completion of evaluations and program eligibility as mandated by state and federal law

At this point, the case manager sends a formal written letter to the student's parents stating that a meeting has been scheduled to discuss their child's progress and a possible Child Study Team evaluation.

The Planning Meeting

During the planning meeting, the core team of specialists must be present, along with the referring teacher and parent. If the child shows apparent weaknesses in speech and language or is receiving English as a Second Language (ESL) services, the speech and language therapist may also be invited. (Speech and language specialists must be present for younger students; this is optional at the middle school level.) At this meeting, the parent and referring teacher voice their concerns, and an evaluation plan is determined based on the scope of the problem.

At least two evaluations, to be completed by core team members, must be recommended to set the process in motion. The specialists may recommend some of these evaluations:

- *Educational evaluation.* Administered by the educational therapist, LDT/C, or psychologist, this evaluation assesses the student's learning strengths and weaknesses, assesses the student's academic level, and identifies his or her learning styles.
- *Psychological evaluation.* Administered by the school psychologist, this evaluation primarily assesses basic aptitude and abilities as related to school performance. Adaptive behavior can be evaluated using a variety of scales to determine the child's emotional and behavioral states.
- *Developmental history.* This is completed by the school social worker in an interview with the parent to determine the child's birth and developmental history, as well as address pertinent family concerns.
- *Speech and language evaluation.* Administered by the speech and language therapist, this evaluation assesses the child's articulation and oral and written language.

These evaluations are generally completed by a core member of the Child Study Team. At the planning meeting, the members may determine that other evaluations are warranted—for example:

- *Physical therapy evaluation.* This is completed by a physical therapist, usually hired by the school system to assess the child's gross motor skills.

- *Occupational therapy evaluation.* Completed by an occupational therapist, usually hired by the school system, this evaluation assesses hand strength, fine motor abilities, self-help skills, written expression, and organizational skills.
- *Psychiatric evaluation.* Usually completed by an outside psychiatrist, this evaluation is recommended for students with severe behavioral or emotional concerns.
- *Vision and hearing screening.* The initial screening is completed by the school nurse. If a problem is detected, the nurse then refers the student to an ophthalmologist or audiologist.
- *Neurological evaluation.* An evaluation of the neurological system is usually completed by an outside neurologist. Students with severe attention or focusing concerns may be referred by the team to a neurologist to determine the root cause of this difficulty.
- *Audiological evaluation.* This is an outside evaluation, usually recommended for students with symptoms of severe language processing disorders.
- *Technology evaluation.* This evaluation, completed by an outside specialist, determines if any technology equipment, such as an augmentative device for speaking or an FM system for hearing, may be necessary to aid in an appropriate education for the student.

The Evaluation Process

Once the evaluation has begun, the team collaborates and collects and interprets results from the evaluations. The case manager is the facilitator in coordinating all information necessary to determine the child's eligibility for a special education program. Guidelines and time lines for the evaluation process are mandated by state laws.

When all the reports are collected, the team decides how the student is eligible for special services and if a learning disability exists. An eligibility meeting is held with the parents to determine classification. Once the parent signs the eligibility document, an IEP is designed to address the student's learning strengths and weaknesses through placement, skills, strategies, subject levels, and classroom modifications. The program is measured yearly through the development of goals and objectives. The case manager monitors the program monitoring.

All students with disabilities are entitled to a free and appropriate education according to the Individuals with Disabilities Act (IDEA), a federal law passed in 1975. A free and appropriate education must take place in the least restrictive environment (LRE) and be designed to address each student's unique and special needs. These provisions for special education and related services with parental and student rights are valid from ages three to twenty-one. This evaluation process is illustrated in Figure 1.1, and page 12 provides teachers with a step-by-step checklist to guide them in the referral process.

Figure 1.1

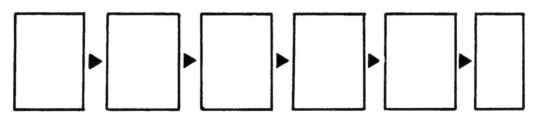

Checklist for Referring a
Student to the School Team

As a classroom teacher, have I completed the following?

☐ Met with the prereferral intervention team?

☐ Implemented interventions over an appropriate and mutually decided amount of time?

☐ Documented the lack of intervention progress?

☐ Filled out a referral sheet?

☐ Brought information to the IRS committee chairperson?

☐ Attended an IRS meeting with information completed on the referral sheet and presented the information to the committee?

Notes

_____

_____

_____

_____

_____

_____

_____

_____

_____

_____

_____

_____

_____

Collaborating with Parents and Families

Part of a teacher's professional success relies on building a strong, open communication line between the home and school. A positive connection between home and school increases the overall success rate of a child's learning.

It is imperative to empower all parents by helping them realize that they are an integral part of their child's education. Parents can offer important insights into their child's study habits, behaviors, past homework history, health, sleep patterns, and general personality characteristics. These factors, which may not be readily apparent in the classroom environment, can have an impact on achievement for both general education and special needs students.

Research on student success in school found that participation in educational activities at home had a positive influence on school success. Results suggest that enhancing parental involvement in a child's schooling relates to overall improved school performance. One reason may be that parents of higher-achieving students set higher standards for their children's educational activities than do parents of low-achieving students.

Encouraging Parental Involvement

Family participation in a child's education was more predictive of a student's academic success than socioeconomic status was. Parental involvement can lead to:

- Higher grades
- Higher test scores
- Better attention
- Increased motivation
- Lower rate of suspension
- Decreased use of drugs and alcohol
- Fewer instances of violent behavior
- Higher self-esteem

Parents may have to become a bit more creative in their type of involvement as the child enters middle school. However, parental involvement at this level is just as important as in the earlier grades. Here are some tips for teachers to share with parents to create an educational environment at home for the middle school student.

Reading with Young Teens

Establish a time and place each day where the family can read a book, newspaper, or magazine together and have a discussion centered around a topic of interest to everyone. Mealtime is a great time for discussion; however, this is sometimes a hectic time, and discussions can be dominated by more practical matters, so try right after dinner before everyone scatters. In the car, discussions revolving around audiobooks encourage listening comprehension skills.

Modeling Educational Behavior

Show your child that there is a purpose to reading and pursuing educational activities by engaging in them yourself. For example, have a favorite book you are reading in plain sight, encourage your child to help you find a new recipe in a magazine or cookbook, explain how to read stock prices in the newspaper while checking your stocks (make it more interesting by pointing out the stock prices of companies that your child might recognize, like McDonald's or Abercrombie & Fitch), or research a vacation to a coveted spot together on the Internet. Here, your teen will learn that participating in educational pursuits has relevance to everyday living.

Guiding Television and Movie Watching

Monitor the television programs and movies that young teens are watching. Find out about the content of the television shows and movies your teen wants to watch before making decisions about teen viewing. Limit the amount of time he or she spends watching television each day. Encourage TV shows and movies that are educational and foster interests or hobbies.

Monitoring Video Games and the Internet

Video games are addicting, and parents need to monitor their children's use of them carefully. They need to limit the amount of time their teen spends in playing games and encourage wise video game choices, such as sports or mystery games. They can use video games as a treat or purposeful recreational activity. In addition to being a place to do research, the Internet is a great communication source. Teens love to come home from school and talk to their friends on the computer. Some of this socializing is necessary for their social growth. However, parents have to be mindful of the amount of time their teens spend instant messaging or chatting on the computer. Use parental controls offered through online sources, and know whom your child is talking to. Again, allow the child this time as a reward or purposeful recreational activity when homework is completed or during a scheduled break. Also, helping your child develop other interests and encouraging him or her to participate in after-school activities will leave less free time for idle chatting.

Monitoring Cell Phone Use

Cell phones are not allowed in most classrooms. Nevertheless, check your cell phone bill carefully to monitor the times and number of text messages that your teen may be sending. If there are excessive texts on your bill during school hours, you may want to make sure your teen knows that he or she should not be texting in class.

Encouraging After-School Activities

Enroll young teens in after-school activities like sports, dance, or chess, or encourage involvement in clubs or other organizations within the school, such as student council or teen theater groups. These can foster healthy interests and friendships, as well as provide structured learning activities beyond the hours of the traditional school day.

Following a Consistent Routine

Set specific times for recreation, structured activities, homework, family interaction, and bedtime. Setting schedules gives adolescents patterns and conditioning for behaviors that foster a productive home and work environment for all family members.

Setting High But Realistic Standards

Encourage and praise your teen when he or she does his or her best, whatever the outcome. Teens are sensitive to criticism. If it is constructive and realistic, it can foster growth. Asking a child to get A's in math when he or she does not have the aptitude is unrealistic and can have a negative impact on his or her self-esteem and cause unnecessary hurt feelings.

Handling Homework

At this point in a child's schooling, the student should complete homework alone, with the parents monitoring that the work is being done and serving as a resource to their child. Sometimes teachers send home specific homework assignments designed to include family members. These help to stress the importance of education and show relevance to real-life situations.

Establishing Positive Communications

At the middle school level, collaborating effectively with families is somewhat different than it is at the elementary school level. Middle school teachers are specialists and are often responsible for at least five classes and over a hundred students in their content areas. Students no longer want their parents in the classroom, as was often encouraged at the elementary school level. Collaboration with telephone calls, report cards, and progress sheets are effective methods of communication between home and school, but all too often they become the only way parents and teachers communicate. Many times a problem becomes bigger because parents were informed too late.

In an inclusive classroom, parents are often needed as volunteer participants to monitor activities and prepare and organize supplies for the students, so it becomes easier to encourage parent participation. The teacher can recruit and organize parents using a volunteer sheet, where a few parents can rotate to aid in assisting station activities on a monthly basis. This way, parents have a productive way to visit the classroom and become involved. Their help in the classroom can certainly facilitate dialogue with their child about school, and their extra hands are usually more than welcome.

Also, if a parent has a particular talent that he or she would like to share with the class that is relevant to what is being covered in the curriculum, this should be encouraged. When the seventh-grade science class is studying animals and their habitats, a parent who is a veterinarian could speak to the students about practicing veterinary medicine, for example. Teachers can also send out a monthly classroom newsletter to inform parents of the activities that will take place that month. This will keep the parents informed of exactly what is happening and will contribute to open lines of communication, making it easier to handle any problems that might develop.

Tips for Talking with Parents

Even the most experienced and enthusiastic teachers run into problems and concerns with students from time to time. When talking to a parent, make sure you employ the following techniques, and always remember that the goal is to solve the problem and promote effective learning for all students in the classroom:

- Before the meeting, make an outline of what you want to say, and role-play the meeting to yourself.
- Try to talk in person. Face-to-face encounters usually leave less room for incorrect interpretation.
- Listen first. Allow the parent to talk first. There is nothing worse than talking about your concerns, only to find out that the parent has a different agenda.
- Always talk about the student's positive attributes first. Then state the problem.
- Speak slowly, clearly, and concisely.
- State the facts of the problem.
- Paraphrase all parent questions before answering. This will foster understanding.
- Check periodically for understanding or feedback from the parent while you are talking.
- Develop a plan of action with the parent that you mutually agree on and in which you are both active participants.
- Develop a second plan of action in case the initial plan does not work.
- Decide on a designated time when you can meet again to assess progress.

Whether to have the student present at these meetings should be decided between parent and teacher individually because everyone reacts differently to teacher meetings.

↶

The process of teaching is exciting and challenging, and it requires strong leadership and interpersonal skills. As with all other challenges, teaching can be overwhelming, especially when children are not responding to instruction. School personnel are in place to address specific student behaviors and learning needs when they occur. Part of the art of teaching is knowing when it is appropriate to seek out specific specialized personnel.

We hope this chapter has helped you focus on how to use support services while building positive communication lines with students and their families.

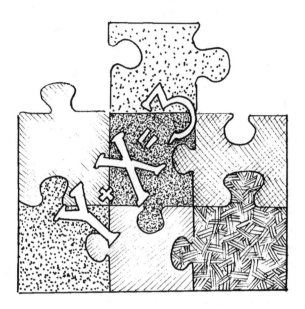

Chapter 2

Preparing for Differentiated Learning

Children learn at different rates and in different ways. This chapter is designed to help you define various special needs as well as learning strengths and weaknesses. Defining and understanding students' specific learning needs will aid in successfully adapting instruction in the classroom, which will maximize all students' potential for academic success.

Working with Core Curriculum Standards

Adapting instruction to work for general and special education students begins with following the core curriculum standards for each grade being taught. These standards, designed by the U.S. Department of Education, serve as an outline for specific content objectives that must be accomplished at each grade level. Each objective includes goals stating what specific material must be covered in order for the student to attain mastery. The differentiated teaching techniques you use must be able to get across these core curriculum standards and content objectives to all students in the inclusive classroom.

Assessing Learning Styles

Identifying the learning styles of your students is important when you are planning differentiated teaching strategies. Knowing their styles allows you to group students effectively for small group or station instruction. Student learning styles fall into three main groups: visual, auditory, and tactile or kinesthetic learners.

- *Visual learners.* Visual learners learn best by seeing information. They work well when they can copy down information in notebooks to use for studying later. Visual learners often jot things down; they are list makers and doodlers and use scrap paper for math and written expression. They like to use maps, charts, and diagrams. They are better able to listen when they have eye contact. Advanced organizers or planners, graphic organizers, which map information in a succinct format, review guides, and highlighting important facts are good strategies to aid visual learners.
- *Auditory learners.* Auditory learners learn best through listening. Unlike visual learners, printed information often means little to auditory learners until the information is explained or told to them. They are strong interpreters of meaning through body language, voice inflection, tone, rhythm, and rate of a speaker. They enjoy a good lecture and usually do quite well in a large classroom setting. Reinforcement of information in the classroom for auditory learners is best done using books on tape or by tape-recording lessons. Other strategies that aid auditory learners are reading text material aloud; subvocalization or whispering instead of silent reading; studying with a tutor, family member, or friend who can discuss the information; or reciting mnemonic devices.
- *Tactile or kinesthetic learners.* These students learn best through using multisensory strategies or a hands-on approach, because they interpret information through their sense of self in space. They benefit from manipulatives, small group assignments, role playing, building, games, moving around, and project-based learning.

Have students fill out the questionnaire on page 19 to help you determine their learning style. Check individual student responses against the Assessing Student Learning Style Answer Key below. See what learning style or styles are most prevalent in each student, and use these results for differentiated program planning. Results can also be shared at parent conferences or with students throughout the year.

Assessing Student Learning Style Answer Key

1. visual	9. visual
2. visual	10. auditory
3. auditory	11. tactile/kinesthetic
4. tactile/kinesthetic	12. auditory
5. auditory	13. auditory
6. tactile/kinesthetic	14. tactile/kinesthetic
7. visual	15. tactile/kinesthetic
8. visual	

What Type of Learner Am I?

Student name: _____   Date: _____

Respond with a Y (yes), N (no), or S (sometimes) to the following statements:

_____   1. When the teacher talks, I write down everything that is said.

_____   2. I love to make lists and cross off items when they are completed.

_____   3. Studying with a parent or friends helps me to remember information.

_____   4. I enjoy cooking to learn math with the class and am often put in charge to organize my group.

_____   5. If I don't understand something, I'll read it "under my breath" to myself so only I can hear it.

_____   6. I took first place with my science fair project two years in a row.

_____   7. I love to read instructions and put things together.

_____   8. I often use scrap paper before writing an essay.

_____   9. I get upset if I leave my notes in my locker to review before a quiz.

_____   10. I like to listen to oral presentations in class.

_____   11. Role-playing characters and situations in literature is exciting and fun and helps me remember the story.

_____   12. I understand information best when the teacher explains it in front of the room to the whole class.

_____   13. I get enjoyment from listening to audiobooks.

_____   14. I understand geometry concepts when I can build or manipulate different shapes.

_____   15. The best review is through team games in class.

Multiple Intelligences and Learning Strengths

Howard Gardner, a professor of education at Harvard University, developed the theory of multiple intelligences. He posits that there are seven specific intelligences that individuals possess, and these intelligences, or learning strengths, can positively influence a teacher's approach to teaching styles and the learning process.

Visual/Spatial Intelligence

Students with this type of intelligence show strengths in their ability to perceive visual information. They usually think in pictures instead of words. Clues to middle school students who are visual/spatial learners are those who take copious notes, enjoy reading silently, are good map and diagram readers, and profit from handouts, study guides, or written reviews. Other clues that students have strengths in visual/spatial intelligence are that these students enjoy putting puzzles together, have a good sense of direction, enjoy building and construction tasks, and like to sketch and draw. Careers that often interest these learners include art, interior design, mechanics, architecture, and engineering.

Verbal/Linguistic Intelligence

These students love to use words and language. They learn best through listening tasks and are usually eloquent speakers. Verbal/linguistic learners usually think in words. In the classroom, these students are usually group leaders, as they formulate ideas very quickly. They enjoy listening, writing, telling stories, and even teaching the class, as they are very quick to assimilate information. At the middle school level, students who possess strengths in verbal/linguistic intelligence may be good debaters. They are also good at interpreting literature because their language skills are often strong. Career interests often include teaching, law, or writing.

Logic/Math Intelligence

Students who possess strengths in logic/math intelligence are able to reason eloquently through the use of logic and numbers. They are good problem solvers. At the middle school level, these students are often eager to participate in scientific experiments and are the first to have the answer to math word problems. They enjoy complex and abstract problems, and often understand higher-level concepts in algebra and geometry. They usually enjoy assembling models, developing science experiments, creating computer programs, and doing research projects. Professions of interest often include computer programming, engineering, science, and research.

Body/Kinesthetic Intelligence

Students with this intelligence strength are best able to express themselves through movement. These students have a good sense of the space around them and use this space to learn about their world and process information. The saying "learning by doing" applies to the way students with body/kinesthetic intelligence prefer to understand. At the middle school level, these students usually have a great sense of balance and coordination and make outstanding athletes and dancers. In the classroom, they learn best through manipulatives, team activities, building activities, role playing, and team-centered activities.

Possible careers for body/kinesthetic learners include sports, physical education, dancing, and acting.

Musical/Rhythmic Intelligence

These students learn best by thinking in sounds, rhythms, and patterns. Effective methods for these learners at the middle school level include the use of mnemonic devices and jingles to study and remember information and to identify patterns, such as in math. These learners have a strong ability to master musical and mathematical concepts. Career interests often include music composition, advertising, or mathematics.

Interpersonal Intelligence

These students have an uncanny sense of quickly seeing things from another's point of view. They are often able to predict the feelings, motivations, and intentions of others. At the middle school level, students with strong interpersonal intelligence are often class mediators. They are adept at organizing group activities and encouraging cooperation and productivity in team situations. They are naturals in using strategies for conflict resolution, communication, and encouraging positive relationships in a group. Career interests often include counseling, management, psychology, and sales.

Intrapersonal Intelligence

This type of student has strong intrapersonal skills and is often identified by peers as the voice of reason in the middle school classroom. These students are able to look at a situation objectively, understand the purpose of an activity, or interpret their roles in relationship to others. They are usually level-headed thinkers. Career interests of these learners often include psychology, psychiatry or mental health professions, or philosophy.

Fitting Teaching Strategies to Learners

It is important to realize that students have intelligence aptitude in all areas, but typically excel in two or three of the intelligence categories Gardner identified. Understanding this information and using strategies that complement individual and group strengths will help you build a classroom that is supportive, nurturing, and able to foster academic progress in all students. Page 22 will help teachers determine individual student intelligence characteristics.

Planning for Students with Special Needs

The main goal of an inclusion classroom that provides differentiated instruction at the middle school level is to provide an appropriate education for all students, covering core curriculum content, goals, and objectives relevant to the specific grade level. Students in this flexible setting will have access to high-quality mathematics instruction and the support they need to be successful, regardless of their learning disabilities, pace, rate, academic levels, behaviors, learning styles, or overall strengths and weaknesses. It is understood that if a student's disabilities are so severe that he or she is unable to function in this least restrictive and flexible setting, then an appropriate program placement decision would be suggested and implemented by the Child Study Team.

Identifying Intelligence Characteristics
in the Middle School Classroom

Identify which type of intelligence is most likely to be associated with the description of a middle school student in the following list. Use the abbreviations in the key at the bottom of the page.

This student:

_____ 1. Enjoys reading silently at his or her seat after class work is completed.

_____ 2. Is a strong debater.

_____ 3. Likes role-playing short stories with a group.

_____ 4. Writes jingles to remember Civil War dates as a homework assignment.

_____ 5. Explains the concept of longitude and latitude to other students with ease.

_____ 6. Is adept at researching the answers to abstract problems for the class when asked.

_____ 7. Is a good listener.

_____ 8. Volunteers to paint a mural for Earth Day.

_____ 9. Organizes group activities during recess.

_____ 10. Is often sought out by other students for a reasonable opinion.

Abbreviations Key	Answers
V/S = verbal/spatial	1. V/S
V/L = verbal/linguistic	2. V/L
L/M = logic/mathematical	3. B/K
B/K = Body/kinesthetic	4. M/R
Inter = Interpersonal	5. L/M
Intra = Intrapersonal	6. L/M
M/R = musical/rhythmic	7. Inter
LM = logic/mathematical	8. V/S
	9. Inter
	10. Intra

Teachers in an inclusive setting can expect to teach students with a multitude of abilities. They need to become skillful at adapting instruction within the classroom. Students with learning disabilities, visual and auditory impairments, ADD/ADHD, resistant learners, students with emotional and behavioral concerns, and gifted students are among the more typical types of student in an inclusive classroom setting.

Learning Disabled Students

Children with a learning disability, according to federal law, possess "a disorder involved in understanding spoken or written language, manifesting itself in an imperfect ability to think, speak, read, write, spell or do math calculations." It is diagnosed as a severe discrepancy between their ability and their achievement in phonics, reading comprehension, mathematics, or oral and written expression. A learning disability may be neurological or perceptual. Dyslexia, minimal brain dysfunction, and aphasia are all considered learning disabilities. Learning disabilities are found on a continuum, meaning they can range from minimal to severe. Students may need adaptations to help them in school, such as extra time on a task, study guides, reteaching, or multisensory strategies in order to master class content.

Visually Impaired Students

Children who are visually impaired are considered disabled if their vision impedes their educational performance after correction. Assessments by specialists are necessary to determine if a student has a visual impairment. Students who have been identified as being visually impaired should be referred to the Commission of the Blind and Visually Impaired by the Child Study Team. The commission can offer the school information regarding specific strategies and teaching supplies useful for teaching these children. Strategies such as preferential seating, recording lectures, using large manipulatives, and writing with thick markers are just a few techniques that help to differentiate instruction for these learners.

Auditory Impaired Students

A student who has an impairment in hearing, either mild or severe, fluctuating or permanent, that has a negative impact on his or her educational performance can be diagnosed as auditory impaired. This diagnosis must be obtained through an assessment with an audiologist and speech and language specialist to determine the degree of educational impact and level of program planning. Strategies such as preferential seating, repeating and restating instructions, breaking information into simple sentences, visual examples, and speaking slowly and clearly are just a few ways to differentiate instruction for these students. If hearing loss is moderate to severe, the use of an FM system, where the teacher speaks directly into a small microphone attached to the small hearing device the student uses, may also be appropriate.

Physically Disabled Students

Students with physical disabilities are often aided by the development of a 504 Plan, a legal document falling under the federal Rehabilitation Act (1973) that guarantees students with medical concerns modifications to their program to ensure that temporary or permanent physical disabilities do not handicap the student's educational progress in school. The medical condition or disability must be diagnosed by a physician. Students in a wheelchair, those with hemophilia, those with diabetes, and students diagnosed with central auditory processing disorders are among the most common medical conditions covered under 504 Plans. A 504 Plan is not considered part of special education. However, modifications to student programs, such as permanent elevator privileges, an additional set of books, preferential seating, physical education exemptions, and use of behavioral modification strategies, are often part of a student's program.

Resistant Learners and Students with Attention Deficit Disorders, With or Without Hyperactivity

A student who is resistant to learning can range from having a typical "teenage attitude" of noncompliance to a full-blown behavioral disability that compromises learning. Students with oppositional qualities, emotional disturbances, stressful home lives, anger issues, bipolar disorder, or poor impulse control can be difficult to manage in the classroom. They often require specific teaching and behavioral techniques designed to engage them in the learning process, keep them motivated, and make them feel good about themselves. Strategies for the teacher may include giving immediate and frequent forms of positive feedback, as well as using constructive criticism wisely.

Students with attention or focusing issues are often labeled by teachers as resistant learners. Often students with attention deficit disorder (ADD) or attention deficit–hyperactivity disorder (ADHD) will get off-track and accomplish very little without constant redirection. Modifications include a teaching style that provides constant feedback, with tasks that are small, interactive, and presented as single concepts. For students with ADHD, a behavioral chart to monitor impulse control with tangible rewards may be an incentive to stay focused throughout the lesson.

Gifted Learners

Gifted learners present a specific set of needs to the classroom teacher and are often overlooked because they can easily accomplish what is required of them. Nevertheless, these students are often not challenged sufficiently. They can appear to be daydreamers or bored in school. Sometimes this boredom can lead to behavioral concerns. Identification of a gifted student can take place through teacher observation and recommendations, standardized test scores, report card grades, and results of diagnostic instruments, namely a test of cognitive skills. Many times a student is gifted and talented in one or two subject areas but not in others. A student can be both gifted and learning disabled at the same time. Sometimes a student is exceptional in all areas.

Strategies in the differentiated classroom for reaching gifted learners include expansion of planned lessons through small group projects, research, problem solving, and creativity. These expansions are designed to bring the basic lesson plan to a more sophisticated and abstract level.

∽

The inclusive classroom is designed to provide appropriate educational instruction to students with various learning styles, strengths, weaknesses, and special needs. When instruction is modified to meet their educational levels, all students can participate in one classroom, learning the same information and accomplishing very similar academic goals.

Chapter 3

Effective Teaching Strategies for Differentiating Instruction

Teaching in an inclusive classroom and differentiating instruction is not a new concept. It can be traced to the time when several grades made up one classroom, and instruction was tailored to the individual student levels. Differentiating instruction may simply be the definition of effective teaching. To be effective, teachers must familiarize themselves with individual student learning levels, learning styles, strengths, weaknesses, and overall abilities in order to plan successful lessons each day. Students who need specific adaptations must also be supported with classroom staff and materials. However, teachers who invest time learning the abilities and personalities of their students will better be able to address their specific learning, behavioral, and social needs.

Tips for Effective Teaching

- Take an interest in your students.
- Establish a positive atmosphere.
- Be clear and concise when speaking.
- Be enthusiastic.
- Develop rules, and follow them.
- Do not bring personal business to the classroom.

- Make learning fun.
- Be an observer.
- Use resource professionals.
- Read background information on students to gain insight into their learning.
- Use repetition.
- Use a variety of materials and strategies to showcase learning differences.
- Incorporate various modalities and methods for all types of learners.
- Be a resource to families and students.
- Include families as part of the support system.
- Stay positive.
- Be a good listener.
- Make effective use of paraprofessionals and aides in the inclusive classroom, and include them in program planning.
- Invite parent participation where appropriate.
- Be flexible.

The Effective Inclusive Classroom

When setting up the inclusive classroom, the teacher must remember that it is a flexible environment that is constantly changing to meet the ongoing needs of the individuals and the group. The environment can vary from unit to unit depending on mastery level. It includes methods that are student centered and reaches beyond the confines of the traditional classroom setting. Reinforcement, review, reteaching in various modalities, and enrichment are often accomplished through small group stations led by teachers, paraprofessionals, or students. Peer teaching or tutoring can be done in pairs to further review information at a slower or more interactive pace. Stations use various manipulatives and modalities that showcase learning strengths and weaknesses. The list that follows gives some modifications, which will enable teachers to further individualize the learning environment.

Possible Adaptations for the Inclusive Classroom

- ☐ Offer preferential seating.
- ☐ Provide extra time on task.
- ☐ Have a student complete every other item on a homework assignment.
- ☐ Color-code items.
- ☐ Mask off sections of work that a student doesn't have to complete.
- ☐ Model problem-solving strategies.
- ☐ Role-play concepts as a review.
- ☐ Give students mnemonic devices.

- ☐ Make learning interactive.
- ☐ Provide manipulatives.
- ☐ Review, reteach, and reinforce information.
- ☐ Use a homework log signed by parents.
- ☐ Have students read aloud.
- ☐ Read directions aloud to students.
- ☐ Use graph paper to help students keep place value of numbers.
- ☐ Use behavioral charts and reward systems.
- ☐ Reward good behavior.
- ☐ Assign jobs to students to promote self-esteem.
- ☐ Develop a review sheet.
- ☐ Allow students to "whisper" while reading independently.
- ☐ Restate directions.
- ☐ Allow students to solve the first example of an assignment with the teacher.
- ☐ Reread the directions.
- ☐ Use a scribe.
- ☐ Use a computer for writing tasks.
- ☐ Use advanced organizers.
- ☐ Use graphic organizers.
- ☐ Shorten homework.

This system is not chaotic because students expect to be doing different activities from their peers within the classroom. Therefore, issues of fairness do not come into play. It is a methodology where teaching and learning strategies are tiered and varied in order to give all students an opportunity to be responsible for individual growth.

Station Teaching

Station teaching takes place when instruction is presented by teachers, paraprofessionals, or students in small groups to reinforce information covered in class. Each station is set up to review class lessons in various modalities, rates, or levels. In an inclusive classroom, a typical math lesson on, say, place value begins in a traditional fashion, with the subject area teacher presenting the concept information to the whole class. Then, depending on students' needs, one small group, or "station," may be designed to relearn the information using visual strategies. A second station may have paraprofessionals teaching information kinesthetically using manipulatives. A third station may include students working independently to expand the lesson, developing abstract word problems. Pairs of students may also work together for interactive learning or to review concepts at a slower pace. All instruction takes place simultaneously. In this way, a variety of learning adaptations and strategies, encompassing visual, auditory, and tactile styles, are presented and reinforced at different levels throughout the class period or block.

Classroom Climate

No matter how the classroom is structured or what information is being covered, the climate of the classroom is of utmost importance to foster an environment conducive to ongoing academic success. According to Deci and Flaster (1995), classrooms encouraging success for young teens are environments that satisfy and nurture basic human needs. The three most important basic needs of adolescents are to belong, to feel autonomous, and to feel competent:

- *To belong and feel connected to the larger group.* Teenagers are most likely to thrive in an environment where they feel appreciated, connected, and comfortable. Take time to appropriately tell students the special value they bring to the classroom setting. Even students who have serious behavioral and emotional concerns should be recognized by teachers and peers for their positive attributes. Often praise and compliments, if sincere, are the very components that teens are craving throughout the school day.
- *To feel autonomous.* Motivation is increased when students feel that they have some control over what is going on in their lives. They are less likely to see the worth of the learning process if they believe learning is irrelevant to their immediate world. Also, they need to have a voice in learning situations. Teenagers respond less readily to adult authority if they believe that they are being imposed on by teacher standards or that adults do not understand them.
- *To feel competent.* Teens need to feel respected for their efforts without ridicule. They need to feel that they are worthy and smart. They also need to see the intrinsic value in constructive criticism and learn to not take it personally.

Measuring Success

There are as many ways to measure success in the inclusive classroom as there are different types of students. Consider a variety of assessment techniques to evaluate each student.

Standardized Tests

Today, measuring success through test scores has become more important than ever before. The results of standardized district and state tests can weigh heavily on a student's placement and career path. With the advent of No Child Left Behind, the increasing pressure on schools to show the proficiency of teachers and programs using test score results causes much stress at all levels. Teachers are often designing lessons that teach to the test instead of using varied assessment techniques as a way to measure student mastery of information.

Formal standardized assessments, however, are necessary and can be very helpful when used correctly. Standardized tests provide information about how students test in particular content areas compared to others at their grade level locally and nationally. This kind of information can be helpful to school personnel when they are making class placement decisions and revamping curriculum.

Traditional Classroom Tests

Traditional classroom tests are an efficient and popular way to determine mastery of subject information. This type of assessment is usually teacher made and subject area driven.

The teacher formulates a two- or three-page document using multiple-choice, true/false, or essay questions, or some combination of these. Students take the test individually during one class period. The teacher grades the assessment and gives closure to the unit. Although these tests are effective, this testing method is overused. Since differentiated learners assimilate information in a variety of modalities, assessments must also be varied to give all students an opportunity to showcase their learning strengths.

Differentiated Assessment Strategies

These strategies allow teachers to individualize the assessment method to fit each student. Students will have varied ways of showing that they have mastered the content, other than a traditional test. This results in increased success for the students.

Student-Teacher Interview

Interviews at the end of a lesson or unit can be an effective tool to check student mastery of information and learning perceptions. Individual dialogue with the teacher gives students with strong verbal abilities and intrapersonal skills a chance to talk about their strengths and weaknesses in the subject area. You can then assess knowledge and progress through discussion as well as offer constructive criticism in a nonthreatening setting.

Small Group Presentations

Assessing how students work together in class to present information is another way to determine mastery. Observe the group as they work together to organize and give the presentation to gain insight into student participation and interpersonal skills. After the presentation, each member of the group receives an individual and a group grade.

Self-Evaluation

Students can become adept at evaluating their own work. Allow students to rate their finished products or evaluate what they have learned by answering questions, completing student surveys, or filling out checklists. You can review student answers against their own opinions and discuss the progress made. Often students are their own best critic.

Demonstrations and Oral Reports

This type of evaluation is advantageous for visual/linguistic, auditory, and kinesthetic learners. Here, students assimilate information and communicate, or "teach," information to the rest of the class. Since these learners are adept with vocabulary skills, it is a great way for the classroom teacher to assess concept accuracy.

Project-Centered Evaluation

Science and math lend themselves well to this type of evaluation. Students create a project, such as a poster or dramatic presentation, that brings together the concepts they learned during the unit. Students with visual/spatial and mathematical/logic intelligence usually exhibit strengths when this type of assessment is used as an evaluation tool. Use previously stated or agreed-on criteria with the class when using this assessment method.

～

An inclusive classroom allows all students equal access to the same standards as well as equal opportunity to illustrate their understanding of the concepts. You can achieve this through your instructional methods as well as using varied assessment techniques. The end result will be a group of students with improved mathematical confidence as they experience success.

Part Two

Math Activities for the Inclusive Middle School Classroom

Chapter 4

Numbers and Operations

This chapter is designed to aid teachers in presenting information on numerical properties and operations in a multitude of ways in order to address many students' learning styles and strengths. The goals are understanding place value, number order, multiples, prime and composite numbers, fractions, percentages, and decimals.

Activity 1: Place Value

Purpose: To explain how number placement defines number value.

Read through the lesson and the adaptations, and make sure you have the supplies you'll need.

For the Main Lesson

1 full newspaper, including consumer ads, real estate, and classified section

scissors

chalkboard

overhead projector

computer with presentation software or interactive whiteboard

lined paper

For the Adaptations

graph paper

6 colored highlighters

index cards

audiocassette recorder

checkers game board

multicolor sticky note squares

thick black marker

timer

large-faced calculator

Lesson

1. Before the lesson, cut out examples from the newspaper of consumer ads for products representing different place values: million-dollar houses, houses in the hundreds of thousands, cars in the tens of thousands, and several items in the thousands, such as high-end computers, TVs, and stereos.

MAGNIFICENT
1,000,000.

GORGEOUS
350,000.

WONDERFUL
15,000.

HI-TECH
2,000.

SUPERB
1,500.

GREAT!
1,000.

2. During class, pass out the lined paper. Students will be asked to copy down the following seven-digit number and label the digits during the lesson: 4,329,462

3. Write the number on the board, identifying the place values. Have the students follow along and label each digit. You may say something like this:

Numbers such as 4,329,462 have seven digits. Each digit is a different place value. The first digit is called the millions place. It tells you how many sets of millions are in the number. If you look at the real estate section in a newspaper, you may see a few houses with this digit included in their price tag. [Pass around a picture of a million-dollar house from the real estate section of the newspaper.] The number 4,329,462 has 4 millions. Label the 4 as the millions place.

4						
Millions	Hundred thousands	Ten thousands	Thousands	Hundreds	Tens	Ones

The second digit is called the hundred thousands place. It shows how many sets of one hundred thousand are in the number. The number 4,329,462 has three hundred thousands. You may also see a number with hundred thousands as a typical price tag on a house. Label the 3 as hundred thousands place. [Pass out additional real estate ads with house prices in the hundred thousands.]

The third digit in 4,329,462 is in the ten thousands place. In this number, there are two sets of ten thousands. Numbers in the ten thousands place are typically seen as starting salaries in the job market or car price tags. Label the 2 as in the ten thousands place. [Pictures of car ads and the classified section of the newspaper may be passed around.]

The fourth digit, 9, is in the one thousands place. There are nine sets of one thousand in this number. You may see these more common numbers that start in the thousands place as price tags on computers or technology items, television sets, or intricate stereo systems. [Ads for wide-screen television sets are excellent examples to pass around here.] Label the 9 as the one thousands place.

The three remaining digits represent the hundreds, tens, and ones place. The first digit, 4, represents how many sets of one hundred are in the number? The number 4,329,462 has four hundreds. The second-to-last digit represents the tens place. It tells you that there are six tens in this number. The last digit is in the ones place and shows you that this number has two ones. Numbers with these last three digits are numbers that you use all of the time. You'll see them on mailboxes and when you spend money at the grocery store or mall, buy lunch, or save money from chores or allowances. Label the last three digits. You should have all seven digits labeled.

4	3	2	9	4	6	2
Millions	Hundred thousands	Ten thousands	Thousands	Hundreds	Tens	Ones

4. Hand out the Place Value Worksheet, and proceed to work with small groups of students on some of the adaptations.

Place Value Worksheet

1. Label the place value for each of the following numbers:

   a. 2,743,262

2	7	4	3	2	6	2
_____	_____	_____	_____	_____	_____	_____

   b. 6,295

6	2	9	5
_____	_____	_____	_____

   c. 567,994

5	6	7	9	9	4
_____	_____	_____	_____	_____	_____

2. Write the value of each number in words:

   a. 7,985 _____

   b. 1,342,681 _____

   c. 11,592 _____

3. Add the numbers and write the place value of each number in words:

   a.   4   _____
            80   _____
           760   _____
         +3900   _____
         _____   _____

   b.   10   _____
           200   _____
          7520   _____
        +61804   _____
         _____   _____

4. Name the following numbers in standard form:

   a. A sixth-grade student's library card number is equal to 8000 plus 700 plus 40 plus 2. What is the number?

   b. What is the number whose ones digit is 4, hundreds digit is 6, tens digit is 5, and one thousands digit is 3?

How to Adapt This Lesson for the Inclusive Classroom

For Learning Disabled Students

Using the notes taken in class and the Place Value Worksheet, review and reteach the information with a small group of students who are struggling with this concept and have difficulties learning. Here are some strategies that can help:

- Color-coding each place value marker using graph paper and highlighters or turning lined paper so the numbers can line up in vertical columns are strategies that work well with students who have perceptual learning disabilities. Color-coding helps students identify and remember place value markers with a familiar medium through association. Turning the lined paper vertically allows the students to have a built-in structure when lining up numbers.

- A calculator may be used to recheck all of the student answers for the worksheet addition problems.

- A strategy that will help visual and tactile learners is to have them actually "build" numbers by layering. Write a variety of numbers representing different place values, such as 5,000, 400, 30, and 4, on index cards. Make the numbers large enough to fill the card. Then ask students to build a number and say that number aloud. For example, a student might choose the following cards: 4,000, 300, 20, and 3. When these are layered on top of each other, the number is 4,323. This strategy is helpful as it depicts all number places in a concrete, visual way.

For Students with Physical Disabilities

This lesson may be a struggle for students with visual impairments or fine motor impairments. Here are some suggestions for improving their experience:

- A small audiocassette recorder may be used to record instruction and later review for studying for tests.

- A student with visual or fine motor impairments may be teamed up with another student to work on the worksheet. It is our experience that students with behavioral disabilities or distractibility issues are great choices to work with students who have physical disabilities. The idea of helping another is a powerful boost to self-esteem.

- A checkers game board using sticky notes is a way to mark place value. Students can write large numbers with markers on sticky note squares and use the checkerboard as a grid.

- A large-faced calculator can be used to add numbers and recheck work.

- Additional time to complete the worksheet in class is essential.

For Resistant Learners and Students with ADD/ADHD

A student with a behavioral disability who is particularly distracted or needs consistent discipline during this lesson may not understand the concepts being presented. If this is the case, the student could go to a small teaching area to clarify the lesson and get additional instruction. Here are some ways to help minimize distractions when small groups are working:

- Clear the area of any additional supplies that may be of interest, and therefore distracting, to the students.

- Keep the review simple and to the point.

- Give only one problem at a time, and ask the student to paraphrase directions and concepts in his or her own words.

- Have the student use an individual whiteboard, which can be effective as well as motivating.

- Keep the student actively engaged and the learning interactive. Active participation is extremely important to assist the student with staying on task.

- Use a timer to help students with difficulty self-starting or staying on task.

For Gifted Learners

This lesson may be expanded by having gifted learners develop place value word problems like the ones in problem 4 of the Place Value Worksheet. This and other worksheets may be used as a guide to start, but other problems can be designed that are particularly relevant to the middle school environment. If there are many gifted students in the classroom, they may work as a team and present two of their favorite problems for the class to solve as a group at the end of the activity.

Home/School Connection

Give students the following assignment to complete at home:

> With your parents or another adult at home, discuss three ways that errors in place value could translate into costly mistakes in the family budget. Create a comic strip or write an essay to present these errors.

How to Evaluate This Lesson

There are many ways to assess the learning of information. In an inclusive classroom, it is important to vary your assessment strategies in order to measure the strengths of all learners. One option is a student/teacher interview format: have a private dialogue with the student, conversing about the student's understanding, participation, Home/School Connection project, and worksheet score. Jointly decide on the level of mastery the student attained for the activity on place value. Once you have mutually agreed on the level or mastery, you can record the grade in your grade book.

Activity 2: Comparing and Ordering Whole Numbers

Purpose: To identify a technique to order and compare number sizes.

Read through the lesson and the adaptations, and make sure you have the supplies you'll need.

For the Main Lesson

chalkboard

overhead projector

computer with presentation software or interactive whiteboard

For the Adaptations

graph paper

colored markers

manila folders or oaktag

1 package construction paper

1 package small sticky notes in a light color

craft sticks

Lesson

1. Write down the following two numbers on the board, and have students write the numbers in their notebooks:

   a. 23676

   b. 237643

Say something like this: "To compare two whole numbers, first put them in standard form side by side. Count the number of digits. Since both of the numbers are whole numbers, the number with more digits is greater than the other."

2. Ask the student to write down two more numbers in their notebooks:

   a. 2454

   b. 2434

Explain that if the numbers have the same number of digits, compare the most significant digits in order from the left. The number having the larger significant digit is greater than the other. If the most significant digits are the same, compare the next pair of digits from the left. Repeat this until the pairs of digits are different. The number with the larger digit is greater than the other. You may want to review "greater than" and "less than" symbols at this point in order to proceed with the worksheets.

Consider the examples already given:

   a. 2454

   b. 2434

Both numbers have a two in the thousands place and a four in the hundreds place. Letter "a" has a five in the tens place. Letter "b" has a three in the tens place. Three is smaller than five; therefore 2,454 is larger than 2,434: 2,454 > 2,434.

3. Hand out the Comparing and Ordering Whole Numbers Worksheet, and proceed to work with small groups of students on some of the adaptations.

Name: _____   Date: _____

Comparing and Ordering
Whole Numbers Worksheet

1. Circle the larger number in each pair:

   a. 3465 or 34734   b. 997786 or 997689   c. 178 or 192

   d. 4435 or 4427   e. 27656 or 2765   f. 63526 or 63519

2. Write which number is greater using < or > signs. Use place value strategies to figure out the answer.

   a. 435_____347   b. 995_____1005   c. 3465_____34465

   d. 176_____169   e. 187_____228   f. 22465_____22564

3. Order these columns of numbers from smallest to largest on a scale of 1 to 3 (with 1 representing the smallest number and 3 representing the largest number).

   a. 48546_____   b. 299482_____   c. 38673_____

      48379_____   29448 _____   38592_____

      49284_____   298420_____   37115_____

4. A blackboard at a diner reads "Saturday Special: A pizza burger and a medium drink for 3.59." If the menu says that a pizza burger costs $1.99 and a medium drink costs 75 cents separately, would it be better to buy the Saturday Special?

5. Sara, Laura, and Alexa wanted to purchase three tickets for a rock concert. The list price for the tickets is $50.00 each. There is one offer for three tickets for a total of $129.80 and another offer of $39.00 per ticket if you purchase tickets 3 weeks in advance. What method of purchasing would save them the most money?

How to Adapt This Lesson for the Inclusive Classroom

For Learning Disabled Students

Notes taken in class and the Comparing and Ordering Whole Numbers Worksheet can be reviewed and retaught with a smaller group of students who are struggling with this concept. Here are some strategies to consider:

- Cut a strip of construction paper as a marker to block out other numbers while working.
- Graph paper and highlighters can be used to serve as place value holders. Write each number in a square on the graph paper and highlight each with a different colored marker.
- Reinforce all strategies by having students solve a worksheet problem using construction paper strips or highlighters and graph paper while vocalizing how to perform each step.

For Students with Physical Disabilities

This lesson may be difficult for someone with a visual impairment. Here are some ways to make learning easier:

- Make a grid on an 8½×11-inch piece of oaktag or a manila folder. Label the columns "ones," "tens," and "hundreds." Each box represents a place value slot. Continue adding lines on the board to represent more digits. Beginning with problem 1 from the worksheet, write each digit on a sticky note with a marker. Place the digits in appropriate boxes on the grid to align and compare both numbers.

- Craft sticks are an easy-to-manipulate visual aid. For students with more severe visual impairments or with fine motor difficulties, lay the appropriate number of craft sticks in each box to represent the number value. Starting from the far left, have students count the number of sticks in each place value slot. The greater number of craft sticks in the most significant place value slot will signify the bigger number.

For Resistant Learners and Students with ADD/ADHD

Place resistant learners in a group most appropriate to their skill level. If they need reinforcement and review, place them with the paraprofessional to learn strategies mentioned and review the worksheet. If they have grasped the concept and are advanced, place them with gifted learners or team up with a buddy to review the worksheet. Provide immediate and frequent forms of positive feedback, and use constructive criticism wisely.

For Gifted Learners

This lesson may be expanded by having gifted learners make and play a numbers card game.

Using markers and construction paper or oaktag, each student makes a deck of cards containing the numbers from 0 to 9. Students can be creative when designing these cards.

Game rules: All players shuffle their cards, and place one card face down. Then they turn over their cards. The person holding the highest numbered card gets a point. Players continue to the next round, placing two cards face down. They all turn over their cards. Again, the person with the highest number on the cards gets a point. The game continues by increasing the number of cards for each round, until all ten cards are on the table. The student with the most points at the end is the winner.

Home/School Connection

Give students the following assignment to complete at home:

Make a poster of a pyramid of numbers, starting with a seven-digit number at the bottom and ending with a single-digit number at the top. Find an ad for an item in the newspaper that represents and approximates the number value. Attach the ad to the poster and present it to the class.

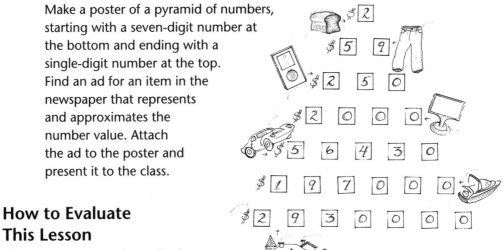

How to Evaluate This Lesson

One good way to evaluate this lesson is through small group presentations. Divide the class into small groups, and have each group prepare a presentation to teach the class how to compare and order whole numbers. Encourage students to include a visual and to be creative by using a poster or creating a game. Score presentations based on participation during planning as well as during the presentation, and give students both a group and an individual grade.

Activity 3: Properties of Numbers

Purpose: To identify and understand basic number properties and how they work.

Read through the lesson and the adaptations, and make sure you have the supplies you'll need.

For the Main Lesson

copies of the Properties of Numbers handout

chalkboard, overhead projector, computer with presentation software, or interactive whiteboard

For the Adaptations

manila folders

scissors

colored markers

small box (shoe box or slightly smaller)

loose change (10 assorted coins)

Lesson

1. Pass out the Properties of Numbers Handout, and review the five main properties of the numbers presented. Write examples of each property on the board. Students can punch holes in this sheet and save it in a binder or notebook for study and review purposes.

   You may say something like, "Math includes rules that govern all operations and problems. These rules are called properties. These properties are like the classroom rules that we have that explain what we can and cannot do in our classroom. The five main properties in math are:

   1. Commutative Property of Addition and Multiplication

   2. Associative Property of Addition and Multiplication

   3. Distributive Property

   4. Zero Property of Addition

   5. Zero Property of Multiplication"

2. Explain each of the five properties, and write examples on the chalkboard.

Hand out the Properties of Numbers Worksheet, and proceed to work with small groups of students on some of the adaptations.

Properties of Numbers Handout

1. *Commutative Property of Addition and Multiplication.* Addition and multiplication are commutative. In math, this means that when you switch the order of two numbers being added or multiplied, the answer does not change.

    Examples
    20 + 5 = 5 + 20 = 25
    20 × 5 = 5 × 20 = 100

2. *Associative Property of Addition and Multiplication.* Addition and multiplication are associative. They associate, or get along with one another. This means that the order in which the numbers in a problem are grouped does not affect the answer.

    Example
    (2 + 10) + 6 = 2 + (10 + 6) = 18

3. *Distributive Property.* The distributive property means that multiplication may be distributed over addition. So if you're adding two numbers and multiplying the sum by a third number, you could instead "distribute" the third number and multiply it by both of the numbers you want to add, then add the products. For example, the 3 in the equation below can be distributed to both the 10 and the 90, multiplied by them, and the products added to get the same answer as you would if you added 10 and 90 and then multiplied by the 3.

    Example
    3 × (10 + 90) = (3 × 10) + (3 × 90) = 300

4. *Zero Property of Addition.* The zero property of addition states that adding zero to a number leaves the number unchanged.

    Example
    54 + 0 = 54

5. *Zero Property of Multiplication.* The Zero Property of Multiplication means that multiplying any number by zero gives you zero. In other words, when you start with nothing, it doesn't matter how many times you multiply it because the answer is still nothing.

    Example
    32 × 0 = 0

Properties of Numbers Worksheet

Identify the following properties, and solve each equation. The first one is done for you.

1. $29 + 0 = 0 + 29 =$ **29**

   Commutative
   _____

2. $(4 \times 6) \times 7 = 4 \times (6 \times 7) =$ _____

   _____

3. $79 \times 0 =$ _____

   _____

4. $5 \times (40 + 2) = (5 \times 40) + (5 + 2) =$ _____

   _____

5. $48,909,849 \times 0 =$ _____

   _____

6. $(2 + 4) + 6 = 2 + (4 + 6) =$ _____

   _____

7. $2 \times (9 + 3) = (2 \times 9) + (2 \times 3) =$ _____

   _____

8. $889 \times 2 = 2 \times 889 =$ _____

   _____

How to Adapt This Lesson for the Inclusive Classroom

For Learning Disabled or Visually Impaired Students or Resistant Learners

Reinforce and review the principles in the handout and on the worksheet. Review and reteach the lesson with small groups of students who are struggling with these concepts. Breaking the information into smaller segments and presenting it in a visual or multisensory format is key here for all learners who are having difficulties understanding number properties. Because there is much information to remember, students who have weaknesses in reading comprehension, attention, perception, or memory can benefit from a thorough reinforcement and review. Here are some suggested strategies:

- Make a set of flash cards out of manila folders and markers. Make one set of cards with property names and another set with corresponding equations. Pass out paper and pencils. Hold up each flash card, and have students either name the property or write an equation that corresponds with the name on the card. Review how each student got the answer. Encourage students to verbalize how they got the answer to the rest of the group.

- Explain each property visually using a shoe box and coins. For example, to demonstrate the commutative property, put one coin inside the box and two to three coins outside the box. Have students add the coins inside the box together and write an equation on a piece of paper. Add the coins outside the box together; then add the inside coin to the equation and solve. Rotate the position of the coins, and write a different equation depending on coin placement; then have students solve this equation. Stress that all answers are the same, but the equations are different. Use the box strategy to demonstrate all properties.

For Gifted Learners

Gifted learners can make and play a game called CADZO. Students can make CADZO cards using manila folders. The cards should resemble bingo cards, with five rows of five blocks and each row having the letters C, A, D, Z, or O in one of the blocks. Students mix up the placement of the letters in each row. Each letter represents one of the properties of numbers.

Students develop approximately ten problems to correspond to each property. C-A-D-Z-O is played like B-I-N-G-O and can be

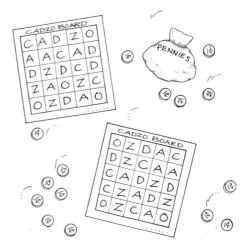

played with the whole class as a review before a test or quiz. Students can pick a caller, who writes the equation on the chalkboard. The first student who identifies the property that the equation represents marks his or her game card with a penny. The winner is the first student who fills one row with pennies.

Home/School Connection

Give students the following assignment to complete at home:

> Bring a bunch of coins to a coin counting machine (found in many super-markets). Place the coins in the machine, and watch the counter as it totals the amounts on the coins. Develop a five-minute presentation explaining to your teacher how this information could be used to develop math equations that illustrate all number properties covered in class.

How to Evaluate this Lesson

For this activity, we recommend using a traditional format for evaluation: a combination of worksheet score, test score, homework, and class participation.

Activity 4: Multiples

Purpose: To define multiples and explain how they work.

Read through the lesson and the adaptations, and make sure you have the supplies you'll need.

For the Main Lesson
chalkboard

overhead projector

computer with presentation software or interactive whiteboard

lined paper

pencils

1 thick black marker

index cards (playing cards or dice may also be used)

For the Adaptations
1 large-faced calculator

oaktag

scissors

2 boxes of different brands of chocolate chip cookies

2 rolls of paper towels or 1 package of napkins

Lesson

1. Write each number from 1 to 10 on a separate index card.

2. Have students form ten small groups of two or three students each. Each student should have a piece of lined paper and a pencil.

3. Pass out one index card to each group of students. Ask each group to count by multiples of the number written on the card until they get to 100. As they count, they should write down the patterned sequence on the piece of lined paper. When students count aloud, they hear the rhythm, and when they count in writing, they see the pattern.

4. When they have finished counting to 100, you can begin explaining the concept of multiples. Here's one way to explain it: "When you count by a number, you are forming a pattern. This pattern is demonstrating a sequence that changes by the same amount, a uniform sequence. This is the concept of multiples. Multiples use the same number to increase or decrease a sequence or quantity. Using multiples can reduce the amount of time you spend figuring out equations. They are a type of short-cut. Multiples are calculated in a variety of ways. Today we are going to learn many ways to find multiples."

5. Ask the groups to use the numbers on their index cards to come up with various calculation strategies to find the multiples of your number to 100. For example, they could multiply the number on the index card by 1, 2, 3, 4, and so on, to

form the sequence to 100; or they could add the number to each previous number until they get to 100; or, they could subtract the number from 100 until they get to zero. All of these strategies use multiples to complete the number sequence.

6. When the groups have finished coming up with a strategy using the number on their index card to find the multiples in the sequence to 100, each group goes to the chalkboard and presents the strategy to the class.

7. Hand out the Multiples Worksheet, and proceed to work with small groups of students on some of the adaptations.

Multiples Worksheet

1. Complete the following patterns to 100. Write down the formula used to find the next multiple in the sequence. The first one is done for you.

   a. 11, 22, 33, **44, 55, 66, 77, 88, 99** _____   **n+1**_____

   b. 4, 8, 12, _____   _____

   _____

   _____

   c. 6, 12, 18, _____   _____

   _____

   _____

   d. 7, 14, 21, _____   _____

   _____

   _____

   e. 6, 9, 12, _____   _____

   _____

   _____

2. Starting from 100, find the numbers in the sequence until you arrive at zero:

   a. 100, 97, 94, 91, _____   _____

   _____

   b. 100, 85, 70, _____   _____

   _____

   c. 100, 96, 92, _____   _____

   _____

3. Your car gets 31 miles to the gallon.

   a. If you have 10 gallons of gas, how far can you travel?

   b. How many miles can your car travel on 1 gallon of gas? How many miles can you travel on 2, 3, and 4 gallons of gas?

How to Adapt This Lesson for the Inclusive Classroom

For Learning Disabled Students and Students with Visual Impairments

Visual and kinesthetic examples work well to show how multiples form patterns. Supplement and reteach the concept of the patterns represented by multiples by making number lines with the students. To make number lines, cut 3-inch strips from pieces of oaktag. Use colored markers to mark numbers from 1 to 100 on the strips. The number lines can be taped to students' desks. (The usefulness of number lines is not limited to students with learning needs. Any student who feels he or she would benefit from this visual aid should be encouraged to visit this station and make one.) Students with fine motor weaknesses may have all cutting with scissors done by the paraprofessional.

Strategies to find multiples can be reinforced with the number line. For example, find the multiples of 3 on the number line:

$1 \times 3 = 3$

$2 \times 3 = 6$

$3 \times 3 = 9$

$4 \times 3 = 12$

$5 \times 3 = 15$

Show students how to use their finger or a pointer to find each number on the number line. Use number lines to complete or review the problems in the worksheet. A large-faced calculator can be used to check math facts before writing answers on the worksheet.

For All Learners

"The Investigation of a Chocolate Chip Cookie" is a fun activity that can benefit all learners on different levels.

Bring in boxes of two different types of chocolate chip cookies. Have students take one cookie from each box, break each cookie apart on a paper towel or napkin, and count the chocolate chips in brand A and brand B. Using the Nutrition Facts Label and the concept of multiples, calculate approximately how many chocolate chips are in each box. Which brand of chocolate chip cookies has  more chips per cookie? Which chocolate chip cookie brand has more chips per box? Does one of the brands claim to have the most chips? Have a discussion with the students and come up with a class opinion on whether its claim is true.

For Gifted Learners

This lesson may be expanded by having gifted learners develop a small-scale map with a key to scale. The key should use the concept of multiples to compare the sizes and distances of places on the map to the map's scale. Suggestions include drawing a map to the student's house from school or designing a map to one of their favorite destinations.

Home/School Connection

Give students the following assignment to complete at home:

> Pick a favorite processed food, such as cookies or chips, and read the Nutrition Facts label on the back of the box. How many total calories and fat are there in one serving of the item? How many calories and fat are there in two servings; in three servings; for the entire box? Bring in the label as well as all calculations used to find the calories for different serving sizes.

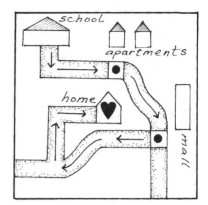

How many miles when
- one inch equals one mile?
- two inches equals one mile?
- three inches equals one mile?

How to Evaluate This Lesson

Give students the Multiples Quiz to determine mastery of the material in this lesson.

Name: _____   Date: _____

Multiples Quiz

Part 1: Understanding Multiples and Pattern Sequences

Complete the following sequences on another sheet of paper.

1. 27, 30, 33, _____. _____. _____. to 102

2. 515, 520, 525, _____. _____. _____. to 600

3. 98, 96, 94, _____. _____. _____. to 0

4. 4, _____, _____ 16, _____, 24, _____. _____. _____. to 100

5. _____, _____, _____, 12, _____, _____, 21, _____. _____. _____. to 102

6. _____, _____, 518, _____, _____, 521, _____. _____. _____. to 550

7. 100, 94, _____, 82, _____, 70, _____. _____. _____. to 4

Part 2: Applying Multiples Concepts in the World Around Us

8. Show two strategies that can be used to find all multiples of five to count to 100.

9. Define *multiple*, and tell why it is used in mathematics.

10. Explain at least three ways where multiples can be used practically in everyday life.

Activity 5: The Least Common Multiple

Purpose: To understand and find least common multiples of two numbers.

Read through the lesson and the adaptations, and make sure you have the supplies you'll need.

For the Main Lesson

chalkboard, overhead projector, computer with presentation software, or interactive whiteboard

lined paper

For the Adaptations

rulers

several plain paint sticks (craft sticks may also be used)

colored markers

Lesson

1. Pass out lined paper to the students.

2. Define *least common multiple* for the class. You might say something like this: "Of all the multiples that two numbers have in common, the smallest is called the least common multiple. For example, the least common multiple of 2 and 3 is 6."

3. Have the students write down all multiplication facts and multiples of 2 and 3 that are less than 20 on their paper. On the board, show them that multiples of 2 that are less than 20 can be found using this formula:

$2 \times 1 = 2$	$2 \times 6 = 12$
$2 \times 2 = 4$	$2 \times 7 = 14$
$2 \times 3 = 6$	$2 \times 8 = 16$
$2 \times 4 = 8$	$2 \times 9 = 18$
$2 \times 5 = 10$	

    The multiples of 2 less than 20 are 2, 4, 6, 8, 10, 12, 14, 16, and 18.
    Multiples of 3 less than 20 can be found using this formula:

$3 \times 1 = 3$	$3 \times 4 = 12$
$3 \times 2 = 6$	$3 \times 5 = 15$
$3 \times 3 = 9$	$3 \times 6 = 18$

    The multiples of 3 less than 20 are 3, 6, 9, 12, 15, and 18.

4. Have students compare the multiples of 2 and 3 less than 20 to find common multiples. The common multiples of 2 and 3 less than 20 are 6, 12, and 18. Now point out that the least, or smallest, multiple common to both 2 and 3 is 6. So 6 is the least common multiple of the numbers 2 and 3.

5. Continue with another set of multiples to reinforce this skill.

6. Hand out the Least Common Multiple Worksheet, and proceed to work with small groups of students on some of the adaptations.

Name: _____   Date: _____

Least Common Multiple Worksheet

Find the least common multiples of each set of two numbers presented below. Use the back of the worksheet to do your calculations. The first one is done for you.

		Multiples of the First Number	*Multiples of the Second Number*	*Least Common Multiple*
1.	8 and 14	8, 16, 24, 32, 40, 48, 56	14, 28, 42, 56	56
2.	2 and 9			
3.	2 and 7			
4.	6 and 10			
5.	3 and 11			
6.	5 and 14			
7.	6 and 12			
8.	6 and 8			
9.	4 and 7			

How to Adapt This Lesson for the Inclusive Classroom

For Learning Disabled Students

Use multisensory strategies to reexplain the concept of the least common multiple. For those who have trouble processing the vocabulary, you can use students to illustrate what the term *common* means in the phrase "least common multiple." Have two students come to the front of the room and discuss the various attributes that they have in common. For example, they both are wearing sneakers or have brown eyes.

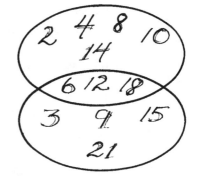

Another way to help students visualize the concept is to have them use a Venn diagram. We've used a Venn diagram here to identify the least common multiple of 2 and 3. Explain to students that they can put the multiples of 2 in one circle, multiples of 3 in the other, and the ones that they share in the part where the circles overlap.

To make multisensory aids to explain the least common multiple, use a ruler and colored markers to mark the following intervals on paint sticks:

1 paint stick marked in 2-inch intervals in blue

1 paint stick marked in 3-inch intervals in red

1 paint stick marked in 4-inch intervals in green

1 paint stick marked in 5-inch intervals in yellow

To use the sticks, begin with a problem, such as, "What is the least common multiple of the numbers 2 and 3?" To illustrate how to solve this, place a red stick next to a blue stick, forming two rows. Show students how to count how many intervals are needed of each number to have the two quantities line up. Then have them multiply the number of intervals by the spacing of the intervals on each stick. This is the least common multiple of the two numbers. (Use a 12-inch wooden paint stick to designate higher numbers if needed.)

Example:

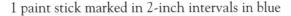

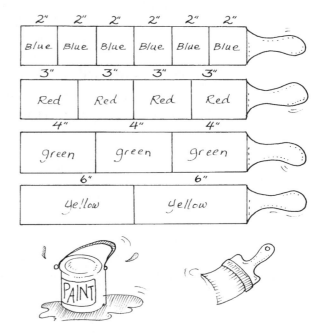

For Students with Physical Disabilities

For visually impaired students or those with perceptual disabilities or weakened fine motor control, use the strategy described above with plastic building blocks instead of wooden sticks.

For Resistant Learners and Students with ADD/ADHD

Students with behavioral disabilities sometimes need reassurance and the acknowledgment that a task is difficult. When you are teaching the least common multiple, it may be beneficial to let the students know that this concept is a struggle for many. Students with behavioral concerns may benefit from teaming up with another student to work on the worksheet. Those who continue to struggle can work in the small teaching area to reinforce and review using the visual aids and manipulatives described above.

For Gifted Learners

This lesson may be expanded by having gifted learners brainstorm and develop a list of as many ways as they can think of where understanding and using the least common multiple can be relevant to everyday life. They can also come up with tips, study guides, or games, or any combination of these, to help the class learn and practice calculating least common multiples.

Home/School Connection

Give students the following assignment to complete at home:

> Go to a store that sells wallpaper, and pick out two borders that you could use in your room. Ask the clerk to cut you a sample of the pattern before it repeats. Some stores are willing to donate out-of-date samples to schools. Measure the walls in your room. Find out how many inches are between each pattern and how many times it repeats. Determine which pattern would have the least common multiple. Write a paragraph explaining the least common multiple as well as which border you would choose as a complement to your room. Bring in both border samples to class.

How to Evaluate this Lesson

Create a handout containing two blank Venn diagrams and two sets of numbers. Have students circle the least common multiple in each diagram.

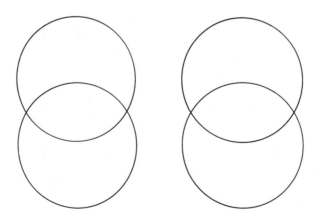

Differentiated Instruction for the Middle School Math Teacher

Activity 6: Factoring, Greatest Common Factor, and Prime and Composite Numbers

Purpose: To understand factoring and finding the greatest common factor and to define prime and composite numbers.

Read through the lesson and the adaptations, and make sure you have the supplies you'll need.

For the Main Lesson

chalkboard

overhead projector, computer with presentation software, or interactive whiteboard

lined paper

4 index cards per student

For the Adaptations

graph paper (preferably centimeter squared paper)

large-faced calculator

small zipper-lock bags, each filled with 20 colored candies or other colored manipulatives

colored pencils

Lesson

1. Pass out the lined paper and index cards.

2. Write the following definitions on the chalkboard, and ask students to write one definition on each index card.

   Factors. Factors are the numbers that are multiplied to get a product. For example, in the equation $3 \times 4 = 12$, the numbers 3 and 4 are factors.

   Greatest common factor. If you are comparing two numbers, the largest factor that both numbers have in common is called the greatest common factor.

   Prime numbers. A prime number has only two factors: 1 and itself. It cannot be divided evenly by any other number.

   Composite number. A composite number is any number that has more than two factors. Example: the factors of 12 are 12×1, 4×3, and 6×2.

3. Review and explain each definition in detail by reading the definitions out loud and giving examples. Start by reading the definition of *factors*. You can also note that factoring is similar to multiplying in reverse. You start with a product, and then try to find as many numbers as you can that make that product when multiplied together.

   Here are some examples you can use:

   - The factors for 16 are 1, 2, 4, 8, and 16.

- The multiplication facts that describe 16 are:
  - $1 \times 16 = 16$
  - $2 \times 8 = 16$
  - $4 \times 4 = 16$
  - $8 \times 2 = 16$
  - $16 \times 1 = 16$
- The factors for 20 are 1, 2, 4, 5, 10, and 20.
- What are the multiplication facts that describe 20?
- The factors for 45 are 1, 3, 5, 9, 15, and 45.
- What are the multiplication facts that describe 45?

4. Review the definition of *greatest common factor*. As an example, show students how to determine that the greatest common factor of 16 and 20 is 4.

5. Read the definition of *prime numbers*, and write the following list of prime numbers to 100 on the board:

> 2, 3, 5, 7, 11, 13, 17, 19, 23, 29, 31, 37, 41, 43, 47, 53, 59, 61,
> 67, 71, 73, 79, 83, 89, 97

Have students copy these numbers on the back of the *prime numbers* definition card. Then challenge students to try to find factors for these numbers other than themselves and the number 1.

6. Read the definition of *composite numbers*. The composite numbers up to 20 are 4, 6, 8, 9, 10, 12, 14, 15, 16, 18, and 20. Write these numbers on the board, and have students copy them on the back of the *composite numbers* definition card. Notice that zero is not in either grouping. It is neither a prime nor a composite number.

7. Hand out the Factoring, Greatest Common Factor, and Prime and Composite Numbers Worksheet, and proceed to work with small groups of students on some of the adaptations.

Name: _____   Date: _____

Factoring, Greatest Common Factor, and Prime and Composite Numbers Worksheet

1. Write down the multiplication facts that describe the following numbers:

   a. 24   b. 64   c. 56   d. 48

2. Find the number when given its prime factorization.

   a. 2–3–11   b. 3–5–7   c. 2–3–17

3. Use your note cards and notes to find the following answers:

   a. Name a whole number that is neither prime nor composite. _____

   b. Name the only even prime number. _____

   c. A number with two or more factors is called a

   _____.

   d. Writing a number as the product of primes is called "writing its

   _____."

4. Find the greatest common factor of each set of numbers:

   a. 40 and 80

   b. 84 and 8

   c. 72 and 20

How to Adapt This Lesson for the Inclusive Classroom

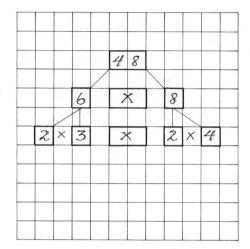

For Learning Disabled Students

This concept is abstract and often difficult for students with learning disabilities. The lesson can be retaught with a small group of students who are having difficulties learning the concept. Strategies such as mapping out the factor trees on centimeter squared paper will help students with perceptual difficulties by keeping numbers in their correct places.

For students who continue to struggle with the concept of factors, use small bags of colored candies or other colored items as manipulatives. Have students group the colored objects in as many ways possible and then write an equation on lined paper to represent the groupings. For example, if they have six colored objects, they can group them in six groups of one, one group of six, two groups of three, or three groups of two. If the students continue to confuse prime and composite numbers, each can be represented in a different color to highlight their differences.

For Students with Visual Impairments

You may need to use large-faced calculators to check and recheck multiplication facts.

For Resistant Learners and Students with ADD/ADHD or Auditory Processing Difficulties

Students with attentional concerns may have difficulties mastering this complex concept. The key here is to break the concept down into single components and provide immediate feedback and interaction. Since visualization and manipulatives are always helpful tools, students who are struggling with focusing issues may benefit from working with the learning disabled students. Students who need less learning support but may lose focus could work together with a paraprofessional or a teacher to identify and correct specific gaps in understanding.

For Gifted Learners

This lesson may be expanded by having gifted learners develop solutions to real-life problems using factors. An example is to design a floor for your classroom.

Tell the children that square tiles can be bought in sizes that are 1 × 1 inch, 2 × 2 inches, 3 × 3 inches, 4 × 4 inches, and all the way to 24 × 24 inches. Using only one size tile at a time, which kinds of tiles can be used to tile an 18 × 24-foot space without having to cut any of the tiles? They use factoring to answer the question and then sketch tiles on the centimeter square paper to confirm their answer. Finally, they can color the tiles to make an interesting design once they figured out which tiles can be used.

Home/School Connection

Give students the following assignment to complete at home:

> Ask your family the following riddles. If they answer correctly, have them explain how they got their answer. If they are stumped, show them how to get the answer:
>
> 1. I am a composite number between 30 and 40. The sum of my prime factors is 12. What number am I?
> 2. I am a number between 31 and 50. The sum of my two prime factors is 5. I have an odd number of factors. What number am I?
> 3. I am a number between 16 and 30. The product of my two prime factors is 6. I have an even number of factors. What number am I?

How to Evaluate This Lesson

One way to evaluate this lesson is through a student-teacher interview format. Have a private dialogue with the student, conversing about the student's understanding, participation, Home/School Connection projects, and worksheet score. Jointly decide on the level of mastery attained for the activity on factoring, greatest common factor, and prime and composite numbers. Once you have mutually agreed on the level, record the grade in your grade book.

Activity 7: Fractions

Purpose: To understand the concept of fractions.

Read through the lesson and the adaptations, and make sure you have the supplies you'll need.

For the Main Lesson

4-ounce plastic cups (one for each student)

6 bottles of different juices

chalkboard, overhead projector, computer with presentation software, or interactive whiteboard

2 permanent black markers

graph paper

For the Adaptations

package of multicolored construction paper

lids from 1-pound coffee cans

5 to 6 pairs of student scissors

assorted colored markers

rulers

zipper-lock bags

Lesson

1. Pass out the cups, and explain that this lesson will focus on showing that fractions are parts of a whole.

2. Ask students which flavor of juice they would like. Mark each cup with the name of the juice, and pour each student a small amount to drink.

3. Pass out the graph paper.

4. Have students raise their hands when you call out the type of juice they chose, and count the total number of students who chose each juice.

5. Ask students to make a bar graph on the graph paper showing how many students chose each flavor of juice.

6. Have students make fractions using the numbers of each type of juice over the total number of students in the class.

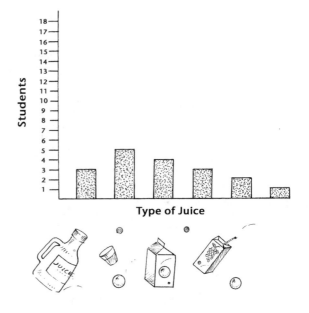

Differentiated Instruction for the Middle School Math Teacher

7. On the board, explain how fractions can be reduced to lowest terms by dividing factors into the numerator and denominator.

   Example: If there were 24 students in the class, and according to the graph, 8 students liked orange juice, the fraction would be 8/24. To put this fraction into lowest terms, you would ask, "What number could be divided into both 8 and 24?" The answer is 8. The number 8 goes into 8 once, and the number 8 goes into 24 three times. So the fraction 8/24 can be reduced to 1/3. Therefore, one-third of the class likes orange juice.

8. Practice graphing other categories of class likes and dislikes, such as sports or music, and turning the responses into fractions. Make sure all fractions are reduced to the lowest terms. Hand out the Fractions Worksheet, and proceed to work with small groups of students on some of the adaptations.

Fractions Worksheet

1. Write each fraction in simplest form:

   a. 9/11   b. 4/18   c. 3/15   d. 14/24

   e. 28/32   f. 12/39   g. 21/49   h. 2/6

2. Find the denominator in the following fractions if the greatest common factor of the numerator and denominator is 3. Show your work.

   a. 12/?   b. 30/?   c. 42/?   d. 93/?

3. In Jackie's math class there are 28 students. Twelve students are girls. What fraction of the students in the class are girls? Circle your answer.

   a. 3/7   b. 3/5   c. 1/2   d. 2/3

4. Which fraction is equivalent to 6/9? Circle your answer.

   a. 1/2   b. 2/3   c. 3/5   d. 3/4

5. Write three other fractions that are equivalent to the given fraction. Include the simplest form.

   a. 25/100   b. 18/21   c. 32/36

How to Adapt This Lesson for the Inclusive Classroom

For Learning Disabled Students

Reinforce and review the lesson in the small group setting using the worksheet, classroom notes, and manipulatives. Making visuals to explain fractions and then reducing them to lowest terms seems to help this group to grasp this abstract concept. Below are some ways to make visual aids and manipulatives to explain this concept.

Fraction Fun

1. Take two different colored sheets of construction paper.

2. Trace a circle on each piece of paper with a coffee can lid, and cut the circles out.

3. Using the ruler, draw lines on one circle, dividing it into halves, quarters, sixths, or eighths. Keep the other circle whole.

4. Cut along the ruler lines. Label the pieces using fractions. For example, if you cut the circle into sixths, use 1/6, 2/6, 3/6, and so on.

5. Use the sections to show various fractions against the whole circle. Label each fraction section and store in zipper-lock bags. Make several visual models using this process. These can be used to represent fractions on the worksheet and to show equivalent fractions. Keep the models in a convenient place to use throughout this unit.

For rectangular models, show students how to fold pieces of colored paper into halves, quarters, fourths, eighths, and so on. Label the pieces to show equivalent fractions.

Students with Physical Disabilities

For students with poor fine motor control, a paraprofessional can aid the student when cutting and folding the fraction models.

For Resistant Learners and Students with ADD/ADHD

Because of the multitude of skill levels when this concept is being presented, some students will need a minimal amount of help, but others will demand greater attention. Resistant learners who seem to have some grasp of the concept can buddy-up with a student who has attained a high level of mastery with fractions and work on the worksheet in pairs. This will serve to keep the work interactive and interesting as the pair dynamics will help keep both students actively engaged in the task. If a short review is necessary for the students to continue, keep the review simple and to the point.

For Gifted Learners

Gifted learners can be asked to develop a survey and graphing study of their choice. They can pick a topic to investigate, develop a student ballot, hand the ballots out in home-rooms and collect them the following morning, and then form an all-school graph based on the survey data, with fractions reduced to lowest terms. The group can then write a short essay explaining their study and the results and present this to the class.

Home/School Connection

Give students the following assignment to complete at home:

> Share some pizza with your family. Cut each pie into eight equal pieces. Graph the number of slices each person ate at the meal. Make fractions out of each graphed number, and reduce them to the lowest terms. Come up with two additional ways to graph the information, and make another graph to show at least one of these ways. For example, how many had pizza with vegetables, no vegetables, or meat? Hand in all graphs, and report your findings to the class.

How to Evaluate this Lesson

Use the Fractions Quiz to test student understanding of the concept.

Fractions Quiz

1. Write the following fractions in simplest terms. You may complete work on an additional sheet of paper.

    a. 30/45   b. 12/120   c. 27/63   d. 48/64

    e. 15/90   f. 35/55   g. 66/180   h. 42/70

2. In 2004, an average of 19 pounds of bananas, 14 pounds of strawberries, 16 pounds of oranges, 23 pounds of grapes, and 4 pounds of pineapples were consumed per family of four in the United States. Graph these totals on graph paper, and calculate the total pounds of these fruits consumed. Express the number of pounds of each fruit consumed as a fraction of the total pounds of fruits consumed, and reduce your answers to the lowest terms:

Bananas _____

Strawberries _____

Oranges _____

Grapes _____

Pineapples _____

Activity 8: Percentages and Decimals

Purpose: To understand that a percent is part of 100; to write numbers as percents, fractions, and decimals; and to use percents in real-life situations.

Read through the lesson and the adaptations, and make sure you have the supplies you'll need.

For the Main Lesson
chalkboard, overhead projector, computer with presentation software, or interactive whiteboard
index cards

For the Adaptations
centimeter squared paper
colored pencils
lined paper
index cards
calculators
large-faced calculators

Lesson

1. Pass out the index cards. Explain to students that ratios represent the relationships between numbers. They can be expressed as fractions, percentages, or decimals.

2. Write the following definitions on the board. Have students copy the definitions on the index cards.

   Fraction. A fraction is part of a whole. For example, 30/100 means 30 out of 100.

   Percent. A percent is how many per hundred or a fraction whose denominator is 100. For example, 30/100 = 30%.

   Decimal. A decimal is another way to write a percent: 30% can be written as .30. A ratio can be written in three ways:

25/100	25%	0.25
As a fraction	As a percentage	As a decimal

3. Explain to the students how to write a fraction with a denominator of 100 as a decimal or a percent. For example, 25/100 can be expressed as 25% or 0.25.

4. Explain how fractions that don't have 100 as the denominator have to be converted to fractions with a denominator that equals 100 for this formula to work.

   Example: In the fraction 2/5, what factor multiplied by the denominator would give you the number 100? The answer is 20: 20 × 5 = 100. Since the denominator was multiplied by 5, the numerator must also be multiplied by 5. This would be 2 × 20 = 40

5. The fraction conversion for 2/5 would therefore be 40/100. This fraction can then be converted to 40% or .40.

6. Have the students convert the following two fractions into decimals and percents individually at their seats. The paraprofessional can walk around the room, targeting students who may need help with completing the facts. Hand out the Percentages and Decimals Worksheet, and proceed to work with students in small groups on some of the adaptations.

   a. 15/100
   b. 20/100

Percentages and Decimals Worksheet

1. Write each percent as a decimal and then a fraction in its simplest form on the lines below each number. Show all of your work.

    a. 8%   b. 24%   c. 47%   d. 87%

    _____   _____   _____   _____

    _____   _____   _____   _____

2. Write each fraction below as a percent.

    a. 14/25   b. 3/50   c. 7/8   d. 3/4

    _____   _____   _____   _____

3. Write each decimal below as a fraction with a denominator of 100 and then as a percent.

    a. 0.86   b. 0.05   c. 0.34   d. 0.67

    _____   _____   _____   _____

    _____   _____   _____   _____

4. You received a 37 out of 50 on a history quiz. Write these numbers as a fraction, percent, and decimal to decipher your grade.

How to Adapt This Lesson for the Inclusive Classroom

For Learning Disabled Students

Reteach, reinforce, and supplement the lesson in small groups using the worksheet, class notes, and the following strategies:

- Use the centimeter squared paper and colored pencils to represent decimals and fractions where the denominator is 100. Go through the worksheet with the students, and have them color the fraction on the centimeter squared paper after they have put the numerator over 100.

- Use the calculator to check all multiplication facts. Do not expect students with learning disabilities to understand a new concept and remember all multiplication facts without checking. That is a tremendous amount of information to assimilate.

For Students with Visual or Perceptual Difficulties

Use a large-faced calculator to check multiplication facts.

For Resistant Learners and Students with ADD/ADHD

To aid in focusing and short-term memory for these students, try the following mnemonic device. Have students write the device down on an index card and tape it to the corner of their desk so they can consult it as they work.

CAMS

Convert the current fraction to a ratio of 100. For example, 2/5 = ?/100.

Analyze the fraction and decide which number should be multiplied by the fraction to get 100 as the denominator. In this case, the answer is 20.

Multiply both the numerator and denominator by the number you got in the previous step to get a fraction with a denominator of 100. In this example, 2 × 20 = 40 and 5 × 20 = 100, so 2/5 is the same as 40/100.

Show your work to a teacher, and check it with the calculator.

For Gifted Learners

This lesson may be expanded by having students find some recipes and convert the amounts of ingredients into fractions, decimals, and percentages.

Home/School Connection

Give students the following assignment to complete at home:

> With an adult in your family, find three articles in a newspaper that use percentages to explain various situations. Discuss why percentages are used in the article, and summarize each article on an index card. Bring the card to class.

How to Evaluate This Lesson

Give students the Percentages and Decimals Quiz to determine their mastery of the material in this lesson.

Name: _____   Date: _____

Percentages and Decimals Quiz

1. Write each fraction below as a percent. Show all work on this paper, or attach a separate piece of paper with this evaluation.

   a. 11/20   b. 4/5   c. 9/10   d. 23/50

   _____   _____   _____   _____

   e. 7/16   f. 5/16   g. 83/100   h. 49/100

   _____   _____   _____   _____

2. Write each decimal as a percent:

   a. 0.160   b. 0.33   c. 0.980   d. 0.78

   _____   _____   _____   _____

   e. 0.640   f. 0.89   g. 0.23   h. 0.550

   _____   _____   _____   _____

3. Write each percentage below as a fraction over 100, and then reduce the fraction to lowest terms:

   a. 25% _____ _____

   b. 56% _____ _____

   c. 80% _____ _____

   d. 27% _____ _____

4. Mrs. Lane counted 25 birds in her birdbath one morning. Of those birds, 10 were robins. Make a fraction of the number of birds that were robins, and convert the fraction to a decimal.

Chapter 5

Algebra and Functions

This chapter is designed to aid teachers in presenting information on algebra in a multitude of ways in order to address many students' learning styles and strengths. Goals include increasing student mastery of performing operations with integers, as well as plotting points and looking at rate problems.

Activity 1: Absolute Value

Purpose: To understand the absolute value of a number and how absolute value applies in daily life.

Read through the lesson and the adaptations, and make sure you have the supplies you'll need.

For the Main Lesson

chalkboard, overhead projector, computer with presentation software, or interactive whiteboard

For the Adaptations

manila folders

several pairs of small scissors

rulers

1 thick black marker

assorted colored markers

large-faced calculator

Lesson

1. Draw a number line on the board, with 0 in the center and numbers from −5 to 5 marked on the line.

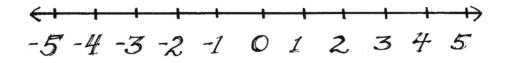

2. Explain absolute value by saying something like: "The absolute value of a number is its distance from zero on a number line. For example, the absolute value of 5 is 5 because that is the exact distance from 0. The absolute value of negative 5 is also 5, because there are five spaces to zero on the negative side of the number line."

   Then give a real-life example: "If today the temperature is 75 degrees and yesterday it was 69 degrees, the absolute value of the temperature change is 6 degrees. If it goes back down to 69 degrees the next day, the absolute value of the temperature change is still 6 degrees."

3. Using the same number line, show students how to find the answers to the following examples:

   a. The absolute value of −3.

   b. The absolute value of 4.

4. Mark the number line with halfway marks between each number. The number line on the board will now read:

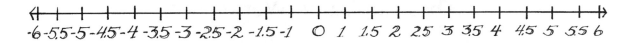

5. Ask the students to find the absolute value of:
    a. −1.5
    b. 4.5

Hand out the Absolute Value Worksheet, and proceed to work with small groups of students on some of the adaptations.

Absolute Value Worksheet

Write an integer to represent each description.

1. 8 units to the left on a number line _____

2. A gain of 16 pounds _____

3. 7 units to the right on a number line _____

4. 100 feet above sea level _____

5. A pay cut of $3,000 _____

6. The opposite of –29 _____

7. 36°F above zero _____

8. A raise of $2,000 _____

9. 6 units to the left of –2 on a number line _____

10. A loss of 6 pounds _____

11. Use a number line to determine if the following items are true or false. Circle the correct answer.

    a. The absolute value of –6 is –6.   True   False

    b. The absolute value of 5 is 5.   True   False

    c. The absolute value of –3 is 3.   True   False

How to Adapt This Lesson for the Inclusive Classroom

For Learning Disabled Students

Use the following strategies to review and reteach the lesson with a small group of students who are struggling with this concept, using the notes taken in class and the worksheet.

- Students can make number lines with manila folders by cutting the folder lengthwise into two 3-inch-wide strips. Have students mark a zero at the center and increments of 0.5 and 1 on either side of center. Paraprofessionals can model how to use a ruler to make even increments. The number line should accommodate numbers to 20 and −20. Students can mark the numbers on the number line with markers and tape their personal number line to their desks. This will help explain most problems on the worksheet. Paraprofessionals should have their own number lines to show the students how to solve the worksheet problems.

- Work with students to come up with other examples that show absolute value, such as a bathroom scale, an outdoor thermometer, or an elevator that goes to a basement level.

- If students continue to struggle with this concept, you can take the group on a trip to the nurse's office. Take along a student backpack filled with books, and weigh the backpack on the scale in the nurse's office. Take one book out, and reweigh the backpack. Repeat until the backpack is empty. Write the changes as negative or positive equations, and then reinforce answers with the number line.

- A calculator may be used to recheck the equations if necessary.

These techniques will also benefit visually and auditorily impaired learners, because there are many large visual and multisensory examples in these strategies.

For Resistant Learners and Students with ADD/ADHD

These students may need some reinforcement and review from the teacher in a small group without extensive visual aids. Talk to these students quietly in a small group, and model one problem. Have students do another problem collectively as a group. Allow students to work together or independently based on their choice and skill level.

For Gifted Learners

This lesson may be expanded by having gifted learners look into how elevation on different parts of the earth has changed due to events such as volcanic eruptions and floods, and explain the changes in terms of absolute value. Have them develop equations to explain the changes and report their findings to the class. For example, if sea level is zero, a flood occurs, and the water table rises 5 inches, the equation for the change would be $|0 + 5| = 5$.

Home/School Connection

Give students the following assignment to complete at home:

Develop a budget based on $20 per week for your own personal expenses, for example, pizza out with friends, a video to rent, or music. With a family member, predict the amount of money you think you will spend on these items each week. As the week goes on, write down what you spend. At the end of the week, compare your actual spending to your budget. How much did you go over or under your budget on the total and on each item? The difference between your prediction and the actual money spent is the absolute value. Calculate the total difference (absolute value) for all the categories. Use this knowledge to create a more accurate budget.

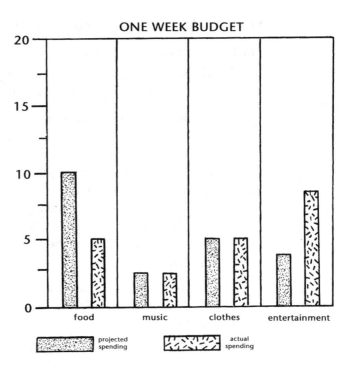

How to Evaluate This Lesson

Have a private dialogue with the student, conversing about the student's understanding, participation, Home/School Connection project, and worksheet score. Jointly decide on the level of mastery attained for the activity on absolute value. Once you mutually agree, you can record the grade in your grade book.

Activity 2: Adding Integers

Purpose: To understand how to add positive and negative integers together.

Read through the lesson and the adaptations, and make sure you have the supplies you'll need.

For the Main Lesson

chalkboard, overhead projector, computer with presentation software, or interactive whiteboard

lined paper

For the Adaptations

two-colored chips

index cards

pencils

markers

number line (made in the lesson in Activity 1 in this chapter)

1 roll of masking tape

portable CD player

2 or 3 music CDs that have dance-type rhythms (current pop music works well; just make sure the lyrics are appropriate for the class)

Lesson

1. Pass out the lined paper, and write the following rules applying to integers on the board. Ask the students to copy the rules on the lined paper.
   a. To add two integers together with the same sign, add the two absolute values together and use the same sign for the answer. For example: $5 + 3 = 8$ or $-4 + -4 = -8$
   b. To add two integers with different signs, subtract the smaller absolute value from the larger absolute value and give the answer the sign of the larger number. For example: $-5 + 4 = -9$ or $8 + -5 = 3$
   c. The sum of two opposite integers is zero. For example: $-6 + 6 = 0$
2. Show students how to add multiple integers together.

   Example: Find the sum of $-3 + 3 + (-5) + (-2) + 8 =$
   a. An efficient strategy to solve this equation is to group together the numbers with the same sign.

      $-3 + 3 (-5) + (-2) + 8 = 3 + 8 + (-3) + (-5) + (-2) =$
   b. Add all of the positive numbers:

      $3 + 8 = 11$
   c. Add all of the negative numbers:

      $(-3) + (-5) + (-2) = -10$
   d. Add the positive and negative numbers together:

      $11 + (-10) =$

e. Ask students, "What rule would you now apply to determine the answer?" The correct answer is "b": to add two integers with different signs, subtract the smaller absolute value from the larger absolute value and write the sign of the larger number. Then give the answer: "The answer therefore would be 1."

$11 + (-10) = 1$

Hand out the Adding Integers Worksheet, and proceed to work with small groups of students on some of the adaptations.

Adding Integers Worksheet

Add the following integers together and determine which rule was used to determine the answer.

1. 35 + 19 = _____

2. –5 + 5 = _____

3. –15 + –8 = _____

4. 34 + –45 = _____

5. 12 + –12 = _____

6. –23 +78 = _____

7. 17 + 19 = _____

8. –6 + 40 = _____

9. –3 + 30 = _____

10. 11 + 18 = _____

Solve the following addition problems that have several integers:

11. –6 + (–3) +5 + 7 + (–8) = _____

12. 7 + 8 + (–4) + 7 + (–7) = _____

13. –3 + (–4) + 5 + (–8) + 5 = _____

14. 2 + 5 + (–9) + 5 + (–8) = _____

How to Adapt This Lesson for the Inclusive Classroom

For Learning Disabled Students

The number line made in Activity 1 in this chapter will serve as a useful tool here. Also, color-coding negative and positive integers using colored markers should make it easier for these students when facts are regrouped to solve equations having several integers. Have students practice in small groups as a reinforcement, and then independently within the groups using the worksheet. Students may use a calculator to check their work.

Multisensory and kinesthetic activities will also help to reinforce this concept. All students, especially visual and kinesthetic learners, benefit from using two-colored chips: chips that are red on one side and white on the other. Explain to students that the red side is negative and the white side is positive. First, have students add two positives. Then have them add two negatives. Finally, have them add a negative and a positive. This is called a *zero pair*: one negative plus one positive is zero. Now have them add a negative and a positive, such as $6 + -3$. They can see how this creates three zero pairs, leaving three white chips, or positive 3.

Here is a game that the learning disabled students may benefit from and love to play. You may find it appeals to all of the class, and, of course part of inclusion is to include everyone in the learning process.

Take small groups of six students at a time, and split them into two teams to dance and learn integer addition. I suggest only six students play I-Dance at a time to avoid chaos in the classroom. The paraprofessional or teacher may supervise the other activities while another plays I-Dance.

Integer Dance Explosion (I-Dance Explosion)

1. Find a spot where there is a large amount of room to work. A cafeteria, hallway, gym, or a corner of a classroom would work just fine.

2. Make a number line on the floor using masking tape. First, tape an 8-foot piece of masking tape to the floor. Then place a 1-foot piece of tape in the center perpendicular to the first piece. This is 0. Add more 1-foot pieces along the line to mark +1, −1, +2, −2, up to 6 and −6. Place each piece of tape approximately 8 inches apart. Write the numbers directly on the masking tape with marker.

3. Make up at least 20 integer equations using the integer rules, and write them down on index cards. These can be labeled as easy, medium, and hard. Do not solve the problems. Make sure each rule is reflected in the answers.

4. Shuffle the index cards in a deck. Have one group pick a card. As a group, they have to solve the problem.

5. Put the music on. Have students state the problem and the correct answer. If it is correct, the team gets 1 point. Each student in the group then has to dance the equation on the number line to get 3 more points. Jump or hop to each number, simulating dancing to the equation. Anyone who misses a step in the equation doesn't get a point. The second team proceeds the same way. The team with more points after you've gone through all the cards wins the game.

For Physically Disabled Students

Students who are physically disabled often lose out on participation in physical activities and become scorekeepers or cheerleaders on the side. Although this is appropriate in many instances, students who are wheelchair bound can play I-Dance Explosion by moving forward and backward with their wheelchair to the equations and the music. Allow one move forward or backward to represent all numbers, as long as the student calls out which number the move represents.

For Resistant Learners and Students with ADD/ADHD

Resistant learners often feel self-conscious about being singled out and are especially sensitive to the opinions of others. To warm up resistant learners, offer the job of operating the CD player or keeping the score of each team until they feel comfortable and safe. Once they seem to be enjoying the activity, encourage them to participate, and allow another student to fill their job.

Students with ADD/ADHD or behavioral concerns may thoroughly enjoy and benefit from this activity because of the physical component. Playing I-Dance Explosion can be used as a contingency and reward for good behavior.

For Gifted Learners

This lesson can be expanded by having students work on additional problems that can be used for I-Dance. Students should incorporate all rules of adding integers, as well as develop three levels of problems (hard, medium, and easy). Encourage this group to come up with multiple integer problems. Students can then write their problems without the answers on index cards, and write the answers on a separate piece of paper.

Home/School Connection

Give students the following assignment to complete at home:

> Write four word problems adding integers and using the rules we went over in class. Design these problems around everyday situations that occur at home, for example, budgeting, food shopping, allowance, cooking, garage sales, or time management. *Example:* Evan is responsible for taking out the garbage every night. Last week he forgot to take the garbage out two nights. Write an absolute value equation to define this situation, and identify the rule of integers that applies to the value. The equation is $7 - 2 = 5$.

> Ask a family member to solve the problems. Bring in the problems and the answers to review in class.

How to Evaluate This Lesson

This evaluation will include using student problems to assess the understanding of adding integers. When students are part of the development of assessment procedures, they often obtain successful results.

Concrete Understanding (70%): Pick 10 problems used in I-Dance Explosion to test students' knowledge of addition of integers. Students who continue to struggle with this concept may use the number line designed for their desks. Students must show all work and write the rule used to determine absolute value.

Conceptual Understanding (15%): Have students design three word problems using integers that apply to everyday life situations.

Student Evaluation (15%): Ask each student to complete the following sentences:

To add integers you: _____

It really helped me when I: _____

I am still confused about: _____

Activity 3: Subtracting Integers

Purpose: To understand how to subtract positive and negative integers.

Read through the lesson and the adaptations, and make sure you have the supplies you'll need.

For the Main Lesson

chalkboard, overhead projector, computer with presentation software, or interactive whiteboard

lined paper

For the Adaptations

graph paper

1 calculator per student

large-faced calculators

unlined paper

Lesson

1. Draw a number line on the board with 0 at the center, and write down the following problems:

   a. $-8 - 4 =$

   b. $2 - (-5) =$

   c. $4 - 7 =$

2. Pass out one index card to each student, and ask them to write down the following rule pertaining to subtracting integers and place it in a convenient spot:

   Integer subtraction rule. To subtract an integer, add its opposite.

3. Pass out the lined paper, and show students how to work the first problem on the board.

   Show the class that to apply the rule to the first problem, $-8 - 4$, add the opposite of 4 to -8. The opposite of 4 equals negative 4 (-4). The problem then becomes $-8 + -4$. Remind students about the rule for adding integers with the same sign together from the previous lesson: to add two integers together with the same sign, add the two absolute values together and use the same sign for the answer.

   The answer to $-8 - 4$ is the same as $-8 + -4 = -12$.

4. Show students how this problem works on the number line.

5. Continue with the second problem: $2 - (-5) =$

   Add the opposite of (-5) to 2. The opposite of (-5) equals 5, so the equation becomes $2 + 5$, and the answer is 7.

6. Show students how the number line can be used to find the answer to the second problem.

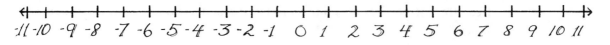

7. Now have students work out the third problem on their own.
8. The answer to problem 1c is −3. Show how you can get this answer using the number line, and demonstrate how to compute the answers to each of the above problems on the calculator.

Hand out the Subtracting Integers Worksheet, and proceed to work with small groups of students on some of the adaptations.

Name: _____   Date: _____

Subtracting Integers Worksheet

Subtract the following integers. Show your work on the lines provided.

1. 34 – 12 =   _____   _____

2. –34 – 15 =   _____   _____

3. –14 – 47 =   _____   _____

4. 4 – 14 =   _____   _____

5. –23 – 9 =   _____   _____

6. 3 – 17 =   _____   _____

7. –3 – 45 =   _____   _____

8. –6 – (–6) =   _____   _____

9. –15 – 15 =   _____   _____

10. 67 – 19 =   _____   _____

11. Write the rule pertaining to subtracting two integers:

_____

_____

_____

How to Adapt This Lesson for the Inclusive Classroom

For Learning Disabled Students

Review, reinforce, and reteach how to complete subtraction equations with integers using the number line, notes, and worksheet problems. Strategies such as color-coding positive and negative numbers work well to aid in short-term memory. Practice here is key so that this abstract concept can be simplified and reinforced. When the students are confident of problem solving using the number line, they can move on to using calculators. They can continue the worksheet problems using and reviewing calculator skills. Students should have their index card with the integer subtraction rule in sight to reinforce memory skills.

For Students with Visual or Perceptual Difficulties

Use large-faced calculators and graph paper to maintain place value of the equations.

For Gifted Learners

This lesson can be expanded by having students develop a mnemonic or other study aids to share with the class on remembering the rules for subtracting integers.

Home/School Connection

Give students the following assignment to complete at home:

> Discuss the following word problem with your family. Show how to represent it with number sentences.
>
> You want to go to the movies and have pizza with a few friends, so you check to see if you have enough money. You have $25 from allowance that you have saved and you think that will be enough, but then your sister hands you an IOU for $15. You borrowed it last week and had forgotten about it. Now you have only $10, which is not enough for movies and pizza. Just as you're about to give up the idea of meeting your friends, your brother takes the IOU, saying that he owes you money so he'll take it over. How much do you have now?

How to Evaluate This Lesson

Use traditional assessment. Students may use the number line or calculator, or both, to solve the equations in the Subtracting Integers Quiz.

Name: _____   Date: _____

Subtracting Integers Quiz

Subtract the following integers. Show your work on the lines provided.

1. $7 - (-3) =$ _____ _____

2. $-15 - 8 =$ _____ _____

3. $-7 - 23 =$ _____ _____

4. $-12 - 15 =$ _____ _____

5. $-6 - (23) =$ _____ _____

6. $-4 - 16 =$ _____ _____

7. $-8 - (-8) =$ _____ _____

8. $-31 - (-25) =$ _____ _____

9. $-6 - (-6) =$ _____ _____

10. $34 - (-45) =$ _____ _____

Activity 4: Multiplying Integers

Purpose: To understand how to multiply positive and negative integers.

Read through the lesson and the adaptations, and make sure you have the supplies you'll need.

For the Main Lesson

chalkboard, overhead projector, computer with presentation software, or interactive whiteboard

chalk or colored chalk

index cards

lined paper

1 calculator per student

For the Adaptations

graph paper

large-faced calculators

2 pieces 8 × 11-inch colored foam board cut into large ovals similar to a placemat

colored pencils

two-colored counters

Lesson

1. Pass out the index cards and lined paper.

2. Write the following rules pertaining to multiplying positive and negative integers on the board, and ask students to copy them down on their index cards:

   ### To Multiply an Integer, Remember:

   A. The product of two positive integers is a positive number.

   B. The product of two negative integers is a negative number.

   C. The product of a positive and a negative integer is a negative number.

3. Write the following multiplication facts on the board, and ask students to copy them on the lined paper:

   $3 \times 4 =$

   $(-3) \times (-6) =$

   $3 \times (-4) =$

4. Ask students to multiply these integers by first completing the multiplication and then applying one of the rules of multiplying integers to find the negative or positive value.

   Example:

   $3 \times 4 = 12$: Rule A states that the product of two positive integers is a positive number, so the product here is positive.

   $(-3) \times (-6) = -18$: Rule B states that the product of two negative integers is a negative number, so the product here is negative.

   $3 \times (-4) = -12$: Rule C states that the product of a positive and negative integer is a negative number, so the product here is negative.

Hand out the Multiplying Integers Worksheet, and proceed to work with small groups of students on some of the adaptations.

Multiplying Integers Worksheet

State the rule that applies to each of the following problems. Then decide if your integer value will be positive or negative. Finally, do the multiplication. You may check your work with a calculator.

1. $(-5) \times 26 =$ _____

2. $(-24) \times 12 =$ _____

3. $13 \times 13 =$ _____

4. $(-24) \times 37 =$ _____

5. $(-6) \times (-7) =$ _____

6. $9 \times 6 =$ _____

7. $(-8) \times 16 =$ _____

8. $13 \times 16 =$ _____

9. $(-7) \times (-14) =$ _____

10. $(-13) \times (-25) =$ _____

How to Adapt This Lesson for the Inclusive Classroom

For Learning Disabled Students

Review and reteach the lesson with a small group of students who are struggling with this concept, using the notes taken in class and the worksheet. They can work with smaller numbers first or mark an estimated answer on a number line before they perform the calculation. For example: $-21 \times 3 = -63$ and so the estimated answer of -60 is marked on the number line below.

$$\longleftarrow \text{---} -100 \text{------} -60 \text{---------} 0 \text{---------} 100 \text{------} \longrightarrow$$

Strategies such as using two-colored counters can be used to show how to multiply negative and positive integers. Using the two-colored counters, designate which color will represent positive and which will represent negative integers. Then have the students write down each of the following equations and the explanations on an index card and place the appropriate counters on a foam board mat next to the index card:

$4 \times 2 = 8$ (positive integers equal a positive number). Place positive counters on the mat in four sets of two to equal eight.

$3 \times (-3) = -9$ (a positive and a negative integer equals a negative number). Place negative counters on the mat in three sets of negative three.

Resistant Learners and Students with ADD/ADHD or with Short Term Memory and Organizational Difficulties Disabilities

Some students may continue to struggle with multiplication of integers. Students with short-term memory, focusing, or organizational concerns may benefit from a modeling strategy that uses self-talk (talking out loud) to mimic the "internal voice" or learning process to solve a problem. Work with this group and self-talk, explaining how you are executing each step of the process. Students can then model you in their "own voice," and the aide can write down what each student has said. These steps can be transferred to the student's notebook for referral when completing the worksheet or working on a quiz or test.

For Gifted Learners

This lesson may be expanded by having gifted students develop additional problems—both word problems and math computation facts—showing the multiplication of more than two integers. The small group could present two of their favorite problems to the class and show all methods.

For All Learners

In an inclusive classroom, large activities that are interactive and fun create a sense of unity among all students. An activity to support multiplication of integers is a game called Trading Paces, played similar to the game Giant Steps. One index card is needed for each student.

Trading Paces

1. Write a different variation of the following on its own index card, representing a pacing pattern for each student: "3 steps forward, 1 step back"; or "4 steps forward, 2 steps back"; or "4 steps forward, 3 steps back."

2. Organize players into groups of three or four students.

3. Hand an index card with a different pacing pattern to each person in the group.

4. Have individual players pace out the pattern written on each index card across the room, and write down how many cycles of that pattern were necessary to get across the room.

5. Each player then writes an integer equation that describes their movement and solve the problem. Example: $(3 - 1) \times 12 =$ _____ number of pattern cycles to get across the classroom.

6. The team that gets the most equations correct and finishes first wins.

For Physically Disabled Students

Students in wheelchairs or on crutches can participate as part of the group by counting one revolution or step to get across the room to represent each pacing pattern.

Home/School Connection

Give students the following assignment to complete at home:

> Using the rules for integer value, develop a song, jingle, rap, or poster design to aid in remembering the three rules. Include as many family members as possible. Record the music, or bring in a poster to showcase your memory tool.

How to Evaluate this Lesson

Make up a quiz of six to eight problems involving the multiplication of two and more integers, and have students explain the strategy they used to solve each problem.

Activity 5: Dividing Integers

Purpose: To understand how to divide positive and negative integers.

Read through the lesson and the adaptations, and make sure you have the supplies you'll need.

For the Main Lesson

chalkboard, overhead projector, computer with presentation software, or interactive whiteboard

index cards

lined paper

1 calculator per student

For the Adaptations

large-faced calculator

colored counters

graph paper

Lesson

1. Explain to the students that the process of dividing integers is the reverse of multiplying and that many similarities exist between the two skills.

2. Pass out the index cards, and write the following rules pertaining to dividing positive and negative integers on the board. Have students copy down the rules on an index card, and place it in a convenient spot with the other rule cards.

To Divide an Integer, Remember:

A. The quotient of two positive integers is a positive number.

B. The quotient of two negative integers is a positive number.

C. The quotient of a positive and a negative integer is a negative number.

3. Pass out the lined paper and calculators.

4. Write the following division problems on the board:

    a. $-45 \div (-5) =$

    b. $32 \div 8 =$

    c. $-72 \div (-9) =$

Explain that to find the quotient, first complete the division problem, and then apply one of the rules to dividing integers to find the negative or positive value of the quotient. Say something like this:

> Look at problem a: $-45 \div (-5) =$. First divide 45 by 5 to get 15. Since according to rule B the quotient of two negative integers is a negative number, the answer is –15.

Now look at problem b: 32 ÷ 8 = . The answer is 4, and since rule A states that the quotient of two positive integers is a positive number, the value is positive.

Now look at problem c: −72 ÷ (−9) = . Divide 72 by 9 to get 8. Since rule C states that the quotient of a positive and a negative integer is a negative number, the answer is −8.

5. If your students are with you so far, you can show how the division of integers can be used in real life, for example, to find the average of a group of negative numbers. Let's say stock that you owned fell 2 cents one day, 4 cents the next day, 3 cents the third day, and 3 cents the day after that. What was the average loss for your stock over that four-day period?

Here's how the problem would look:

$$\frac{(-2) + (-4) + (-3) + (-3)}{4} =$$

Step 1: Add the four negative numbers to get −12.

Step 2: Divide the sum of the negative numbers by 4. (−12) ÷ 4 =

Step 3: Use rule C (the quotient of a positive and a negative integer is a negative integer) to determine that the answer is a negative number: −3.

Hand out the Dividing Integers Worksheet, and proceed to work with small groups of students on some of the adaptations.

Dividing Integers Worksheet

Use a calculator to solve the following division problems. Then state the rule that applies to the quotient's integer value.

1. $240 \div (-6) =$ _____   _____

2. $-105 \div 35 =$ _____   _____

3. $36 \div 9 =$ _____   _____

4. $-56 \div -7 =$ _____   _____

5. $49 \div (-7) =$ _____   _____

Use a calculator to find the following averages. Show your work, and state the rule that applies to the quotient's integer value.

6. $\dfrac{(-4) + (-8) + (-2) + (-6)}{4} =$ _____   _____

7. $\dfrac{(-5) + (-15) + (-250) + (-55) + (-20)}{5} =$ _____   _____

8. $\dfrac{(-4) + (-62) + (-24) + (-2) + (-44)}{4} =$ _____   _____

How to Adapt This Lesson for the Inclusive Classroom

For Learning Disabled Students

Review and reteach this lesson with a small group of students who are struggling with this concept, using the notes taken in class and the worksheet. Strategies such as color-coding negative and positive numbers can be used to differentiate the operations and reinforce the rules. For instance, red counters can represent negative numbers and white, positive numbers. For the problem $-6 \div 2 =$, students would place 6 red counters in front of them, then separate, or divide, them into two groups. This would result in 3 reds in each pile, representing -3.

For Resistant Learners and Students with ADD/ADHD

Students with short-term memory, focusing, or organizational concerns may benefit from a modeling strategy, which uses self-talk, or talking out loud, to mimic the "internal voice" or learning process to solve a problem. Work with this group and self-talk, explaining how you are going to execute each step of the process. Students can then model the teacher in their "own voice," and the aide can write down what each student has said. These steps can then be transferred to the students' notebooks so they can refer to them as they complete the worksheet or work on a quiz or test.

For Students with Visual or Perceptual Disabilities

These students may have difficulties keeping numbers lined up correctly. Graph paper and large-faced calculators can aid students who struggle with perceptual and organizational skills.

For Gifted Learners

This lesson may be expanded by having gifted learners develop a game that will reinforce the concept. You could give them ideas to start or have them create one entirely on their own. Perhaps students start out with a certain number of positive chips, and as they move around the board, they land on spaces where they take additional positive or negative chips. Another game idea could involve dice, with red representing negative and white representing positive.

For All Learners

To review all rules presented relative to integers, students can play Integer Hold 'Em, a card game that reviews all four operations.

Integer Hold'Em

1. Divide students into groups of four, and give each student a piece of graph paper and a pencil.
2. Take four of the integer rule cards prepared in class from each student to make a deck.
3. Shuffle the deck, and have the first player pick a card.
4. The first player makes up a problem that describes one of the rules on the card and shows the problem to the other players.

5. All students privately solve the equation, and write down the answer and which rule it represents.

6. The first player picks the player to his or her immediate right. If that person got the answer, the first player gets a point and picks the next player, and if the person did not get the right answer, the first player draws another card and makes up another equation. This time the player may choose another player of his or her choice to solve the problem. Discard used cards.

7. After all the rule cards have been used, play ends. The winner is the player with the most points.

Home/School Connection

Give students the following assignment to complete at home:

> Over one week, track the time the sun sets. Record the time each night loses or gains and record this number as a negative or positive integer. For example, if the sun set at 5:00 P.M. today, and tomorrow the sun sets at 5:03 P.M. the time loss would be 3 minutes, or (–3). In reverse, if the sun sets at 4:57, the gain would be 3 minutes or (+3). Average the time loss over a one week and graph the results. Bring the graph to class.

How to Evaluate This Lesson

This uses small group evaluation. Since this lesson completes the four operations using integers—addition, subtraction, multiplication, and division—a mixed worksheet reviewing all items and rules can be a useful tool. A teacher-made test incorporating at least four to five integer problems for each operation would be optimum. The teacher can pull items from all four worksheets to make a unit test. Students can work in small groups to answer the test questions and use the strategies that help them to solve problems most effectively. Decide how to group the students ahead of time based on their abilities, and encourage those who would benefit to use items such as manipulatives, number lines, graph paper, and calculators.

Activity 6: Plotting Points on a Coordinate Plane

Purpose: To understand and be able to plot coordinates on a coordinate plane.

Read through the lesson and the adaptations, and make sure you have the supplies you'll need.

For the Main Lesson

chalkboard, overhead projector, computer with presentation software, or interactive whiteboard

graph paper or centimeter squared paper

For the Adaptations

colored pencils or crayons

checkerboard

small sticky notes

Lesson

1. Pass out the graph paper, and begin the lesson by asking the students which month they were born in. Tally the number of students born in each month.

2. Assign a numerical value for each month to plot on a coordinate plane—for example:

Value of X	Month	Value of Y (number of students born in each month)
–6	July	2
–5	August	0
–4	September	4
–3	October	0
–2	November	5
–1	December	4
0	January	2
1	February	1
2	March	0
3	April	3
4	May	5
5	June	2

3. Explain that these values can be used to create coordinates (a pair of numbers used to specify a point in space) and plot them on a coordinate plane (a plane divided by a horizontal number line, called the x-axis, and a vertical number line, called the y-axis). The coordinates are written as follows: (value of x, value of y)

   In this example, the value of x is the month that the students were born in. The value of y is the number of students born in each month. This information can be summarized as a collection of ordered points or coordinates. The points are as follows:

   (–6,2), (–5,0), (–4,4), (–3, 0), (–2,5), (–1,4), (0,2), (1,1), (2,0), (3,3), (4,5), (5,2)

4. Draw the *x*- and
   y-axes of a coordinate plane on the board, and ask the students to copy this diagram onto their graph paper. Paraprofessionals can walk around the room to make sure the graphs are accurate.

   The horizontal axis is *x*, or the months of the year.

   The vertical axis is *y*, or the amount of students born each month.

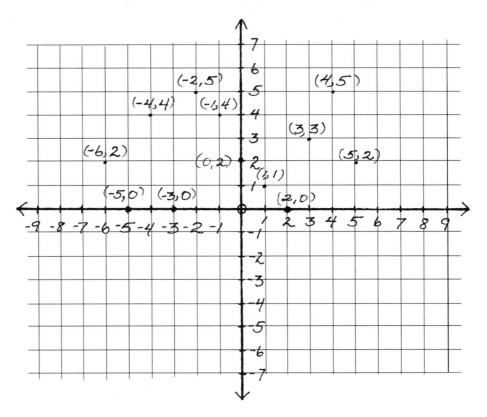

5. Show the students how to plot the first set of coordinates (−6,2) on the plane. Continue with two or three additional examples. When students are comfortable with the concept, have them finish plotting the rest of the points on the graph.

   Hand out the Plotting Points on a Coordinate Plane Worksheet, and proceed to work with small groups of students on some of the adaptations.

   Finished graphs from all student groups and from the Home/School Connection can be mounted on construction paper and displayed around the room.

Name: _____   Date: _____

Plotting Points on a Coordinate Plane Worksheet

Plot the following points on the graph paper below.

1. $x = -2, -1, 0, 1, 2$
    $y = 8, 7, 6, 5, 3$

2. $x = 1, 2, 3, 4, 5, 6$
    $y = -9, -8, -7, 5, 6, 10$

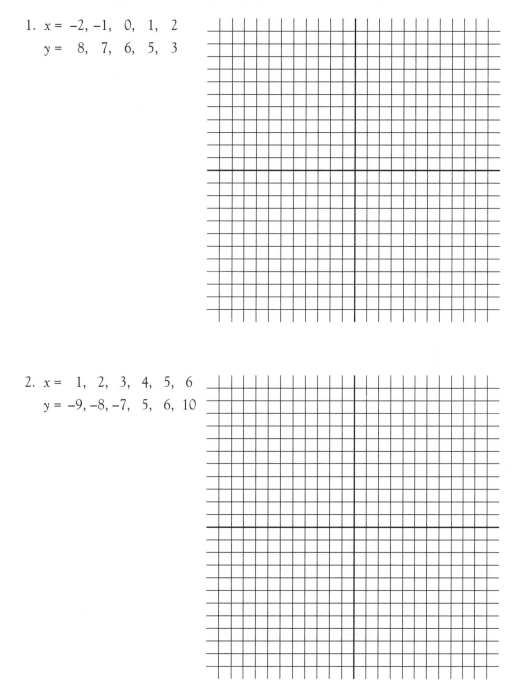

How to Adapt This Lesson for the Inclusive Classroom

For Learning Disabled Students

Review and reteach the lesson in a small group of students who are struggling with this concept, using the notes taken in class and the worksheet. Use colored pencils when plotting the points and pick a different color for the *x* and the *y* values.

For students who are still struggling with the concept of plotting points, reteach the concept by using the letters in their first name as the *x* points and last name as *y* points. This will make the information very easy to remember, and students can concentrate on making the graph. Another memory clue that can be helpful is, *You have to walk over to the elevator (x-axis) before you can go up to your floor (y-axis)*. Students who are struggling may need additional time and several trials to reach mastery of this concept.

Assign the letters of the student's first name as the *x* value–for example:

$$J = -3$$
$$O = -2$$
$$A = -1$$
$$N = 0$$
$$I = -1$$
$$E = -2$$

Assign the letters of the student's last name as the *y* value.

$$D = 3$$
$$A = 2$$
$$M = 1$$
$$I = 0$$
$$C = -1$$
$$O = -2$$

Write the coordinates and plot them on a plane:

(–3,3), (–2,2), (–1,1), (0,0), (1,–1), (2,–2)

Use the colored pencils, and pick a color code for both *x* and *y* values.

For Students with Visual Impairment

Using graph paper may be a struggle for students with visual impairments. Larger-sized graph paper may be used to give students a larger area to work with. A checkerboard is also a natural way to represent a coordinate plane. Use small sticky notes or game pieces to mark off the coordinate points from the worksheet on the game board.

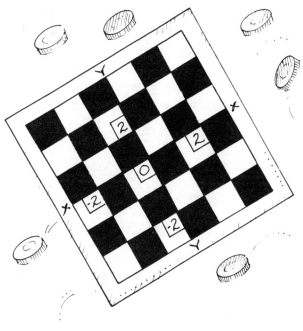

For Resistant Learners and Students with ADD/ADHD

A student with a behavioral disability who is particularly distracted or needs constant discipline during the lesson may not understand the complex concept of plotting coordinates. Here is where knowing your students' abilities serves as a great classroom management tool. Resistant learners or students who have difficulties focusing should be placed in a group appropriate to their mastery level. Since the activity is interactive, most students with behavioral concerns will be focused if their learning needs are met. Students who are still struggling with understanding may need to go to one or more teaching areas before they are comfortable with this concept.

For Gifted Learners

This lesson may be expanded by having gifted learners design coordinates that can be connected to make a puzzle, drawing, or logo. Coordinates can be listed on a sheet of paper and then graphed on centimeter squared paper. When points are plotted, students can then color their artwork.

Home/School Connection

Give students the following assignment to complete at home:

> Using graph paper, plot the coordinates listed below on a coordinate plane. Connect the dots to identify the mystery item. Color and label the item and bring it in to class. Clue: A favorite food of middle and high school students

> Coordinates:

> (0–20), (13,1), (14,1), (15,2), (15,3), (14,4), (10,6), (4,7), (–4,7), (–10,6), (–14,4), (–15,3), (–15,2), (–14,1), (–13,1), (–10,3), (–4,4), (4,4), (10,3)

How to Evaluate This Lesson

Use traditional assessment. When teaching graphs and plotting points, it is important to determine if students understand the value of x and y coordinates. Have students work individually and determine x and y values to plot points on a coordinate plane. Allow them to use colored pencils, markers, or any multisensory tools that were used during the learning process. Each student explains his or her completed graph to the teacher, paraprofessional, or teacher's aide.

Activity 7: Integers and Exponents

Purpose: To show how to raise an integer to an exponential power.

Read through the lesson and the adaptations, and make sure you have the supplies you'll need.

For the Main Lesson

chalkboard, overhead projector, computer with presentation software, or interactive whiteboard

lined paper

For the Adaptations

assorted markers

calculators

Lesson

1. Pass out the lined paper.

2. Explain how to raise a positive number to a power. For example, you might say: "To raise a positive number to a power, multiply the number, which is called the base number, by itself by the amount of times shown in the exponent." For example, 4^2 equals $4 \times 4 = 16$ and 5^3 equals $5 \times 5 \times 5 = 125$.

3. Have students practice with the following two problems:

    a. 9^3

    b. 2^6

4. When students are finished solving the problems, review them on the board with the students.

    a. $9^3 = 9 \times 9 \times 9 = 729$

    b. $2^6 = 2 \times 2 \times 2 \times 2 \times 2 \times 2 = 64$

5. Now explain how to evaluate an expression that has a negative base number and an exponent. You might say something like: "To raise a negative number to a power, multiply the number, which is called the base number, by itself by the amount of times shown in the exponent." For example: $(-2)^4 = (-2) \times (-2) \times (-2) \times (-2) = 64$.

    Work the equations:

    $-2 \times -2 = 4$

    $4 \times -2 = -8$

    $-8 \times -2 = 16$

6. Have students practice with the following three problems:

    a. $(-5)^4$

    b. $(-6)^3$

    c. $-(-2)^5$

You may want to ask students to volunteer to come to the board to write and explain their answers.

7. Help students as necessary in finding the answers to the problems above:

    a. $(-5)^4 = (-5) \times (-5) \times (-5) \times (-5) = 625$

    b. $(-6)^3 = (-6) \times (-6) \times (-6) = -216$

    c. $-(-2)^5 = -(-2) \times (-2) \times (-2) \times (-2) \times (-2) = -(-32) = 32$

Hand out the Integers and Exponents Worksheet, and proceed to work with small groups of students on some of the adaptations.

Name: _____   Date: _____

Integers and Exponents Worksheet

1. Write the following expressions as powers.

   a. $(-4) \times (-4) \times (-4) \times (-4) \times (-4) \times (-4)$ = _____

   b. $(-6) \times (-6) \times (-6) \times (-6)$ = _____

   c. $(-5) \times (-5) \times (-5) \times (-5) \times (-5)$ = _____

   d. $(-2) \times (-2) \times (-2) \times (-2) \times (-2) \times (-2)$ = _____

2. Evaluate the following expressions. Show all your work.

   a. $(-9)^4$ _____

   b. $4 \times (-3)^5$ = _____

   c. $(-7)^3$ = _____

   d. $(-5)^2 - (-4)$ = _____

How to Adapt This Lesson for the Inclusive Classroom
For Learning Disabled Students

Using notes taken in class and the worksheet, review and reteach the lesson with a small group of students who are struggling with this concept. The number line can be used here as a visual tool to show the movement of positive and negative numbers with exponents. Powers can be highlighted with colored markers. Students who struggle with short-term memory may find a mnemonic strategy helpful as a memory tool.

P-O-W-E-R Strategy

P = Power. That is, evaluate the exponent to see if it is a negative or positive number.

O = Organize the operation.

W = Work the expression to solve the equation.

E = Evaluate your answer.

R = Recheck all computations using a calculator.

Use a modeling strategy for students who have organizational, focusing, and short-term memory weaknesses. Model the P-O-W-E-R strategy by using self-talk to complete the steps and solve the expressions. Students can repeat them until they are comfortable with the process.

For Gifted Learners

Using the numbers 1 to 9, have students create the largest and smallest number. Each number may be used only once in a problem, and the number can be made positive or negative. In the problem, they must either have a negative coefficient or exponent. Based on these rules, the largest number is $-9^8 = 4,782,969$.

Home/School Connection

Give students the following assignment to complete at home:

> Play the card game Exponent Draw with a member of your family. Record your trickiest problem and how you solved it, and bring your explanation to class.

Exponent Draw

1. Remove the face cards and jokers from two decks of cards. Aces are low in this game. Red signifies a negative number and black a positive number.
2. One deck of cards is for the coefficient and the other for the exponent. Let's imagine that you draw a red 3 from the first (coefficient) pile and a black 2 from the second (exponent) pile. Your problem to solve would be $(-3)^2 = (-3) \times (-3) = 9$. Then the next player does the same.
3. The player with the greater value wins that round and keeps the four cards. Play until you finish the decks.

How to Evaluate This Lesson

Use a small group evaluation. Students work in groups of four to create an oral presentation or poster to present to the class. The assignment is to explain exponents to a student who was absent when this material was presented. The grade for this evaluation will consist of two parts: the end product and group participation. Have the students turn in a personal evaluation of how they believe they contributed to the group.

Activity 8: Rates

Purpose: To understand and solve practical problems using rates.

Read through the lesson and the adaptations, and make sure you have the supplies you'll need.

For the Main Lesson

chalkboard, overhead projector, computer with presentation software, or interactive whiteboard

lined paper

For the Adaptations

markers

basketballs

jump ropes

watch with a second hand

paddle and ball sets

large ball

use of gym or outdoor basketball court

calculators

large-faced calculator

Lesson

1. Pass out the lined paper, and begin the lesson by giving the students the definition of *rate*. Write the following definition on the board, and ask the students to copy it down on the lined paper.

   Rate: A comparison of different measurements that is expressed as a fraction where the numerator and denominator have different units.

2. Give the students an example of a rate, such as the speed of a car, which is expressed as miles per hour, or distance/time, that is, the amount of distance traveled in a certain amount of time. For example, if a car is traveling 15 miles per hour in a school zone, then in 1 hour, it will have gone exactly 15 miles.

   A rate with a denominator of 1 is called a *unit rate*.

3. When the denominator is not 1, you find the rate by dividing both the numerator and denominator by the denominator.

   Example:

   Jackie baby-sat for 2 hours on Saturday and received $10. What was her hourly rate?

Amount paid	10.00
Time baby-sitting	2 hours

Divide the numerator and denominator by 2 to find the hourly rate.

$10.00 ÷ 2 = $5.00

2 hours ÷ 2 = 1 hour

The hourly rate is $5.00 per hour.

Example:

John can run 1 mile in 9 minutes. How far can he run in 36 minutes?

$$\frac{1 \text{ mile}}{9 \text{ minutes}} = \frac{x \text{ miles}}{36 \text{ minutes}}$$

$1 \times 36 = 9x$

$36 = 9x$

$36 ÷ 9 = x$

$4 = x$

John can run 4 miles in 36 minutes.

4. Give some more real-life examples of how rate is used, such as determining wages (dollars per hour, per week, or per year), traveling (miles per hour), balancing budgets (money spent per month), comparing items at the grocery store (dollars per pound), exercising (heartbeats per minute), or weather (inches of rain or snow in an hour).

Hand out the Rates Worksheet, and proceed to work with small groups of students on some of the adaptations.

Name: _____   Date: _____

Rates Worksheet

Answer the following rate problems. Show all your work on the worksheet.

1. It rains 30 inches in 6 hours. Find the rate of rain for 1 hour, 2 hours, 3 hours, 4 hours, and 5 hours.

2. You earned $75 for watching the neighbor's dog for 5 days. Find your daily wage.

3. You were given 20 social studies questions to complete in 45 minutes. To pace yourself, find the rate at which you should answer each question.

4. Young adults need approximately 14,000 calories per week to have energy and keep body functions working properly. Find out how many calories you would have consumed for 1 day, 2 days, and 5 days if you were consuming calories at this rate. How many calories would you have consumed in one month?

5. Jon can keyboard approximately 350 words in 7 minutes. How many words can Jon type per minute? How many words can Jon type in 5 minutes? How long would it take Jon to type a 1,000-word term paper for the eighth-grade final project?

How to Adapt This Lesson for the Inclusive Classroom

For Learning Disabled Students

Review and reteach the lesson with a small group of students who are struggling with this concept, using the notes taken in class and the worksheet. Making a rate chart by folding a sheet of lined paper into four or five columns may be useful as a memory and organizational tool. For example:

Heartbeat	80					
Minutes	1	2	3	4	5	6

Words read	50					
Minutes	1	2	3	4	5	6

The paraprofessional can add to these categories and assist students in setting up the equations to solve each problem. Students can then check their work with a calculator.

For Students with Visual Impairments

These students can use a large-faced calculator to check their work and also complete the rate chart described above using thick markers.

For Resistant Learners and Students with ADD/ADHD

If the student seems to understand the work presented, team the student up with another, and allow them to complete the worksheet in pairs. A student who is struggling with the concept can also complete the rate chart explained above and may benefit from the review and reinforcement provided to students with learning disabilities.

For All Learners

The concept of rate lends itself well to a group physical activity in which all students may participate. This activity will take one full class period and will be in addition to all other instruction. All class members will need to wear sneakers to school that day because the activity will take place in the gym. Have basketballs, jump ropes, a paddle, balls, and a watch with a second hand available. Students will need to bring their notebook and a pencil. You may want to videotape this activity to use as part of the lesson evaluation.

1. Organize the students into four groups. Two groups will be given jump ropes, and the other two will start with basketballs.

2. Have students form pairs. Explain that when you say "Go," one of the students in each pair should begin jumping rope or shooting baskets for 1 minute. The other student in the pair should count the number of jumps or the number of baskets attempted and the number of baskets made.

3. After 1 minute, say "Stop," and all students should stop what they're doing.

4. Each pair in the two basketball groups records the rate of shots attempted and shots scored for 1 minute. Each pair in the two jump rope groups record the number of jumps per minute

5. When everyone is done recording the results, have each pair repeat the exercise, with the same students shooting the baskets and doing the jumping, but this time for 3 minutes. Have students record the results.

6. Have students in each pair switch places and repeat the exercise to find the rates for 1 minute and 3 minutes.

7. When all members of all groups have had their turn, the groups change equipment and repeat the activity. At the end of the activity, all students should have a rate for basketball shooting and jumping rope (shots/minute, baskets/minute, and jumps/minute). They will use these rates when you are evaluating the lesson.

For Students with Physical Disabilities

Students who are wheelchair bound can go close to the basket and shoot. If a basketball hoop is still too high, laundry baskets may be used for shooting. Instead of jump rope, students with physical disabilities can use a paddle and ball to find ball-bouncing rates. If this is difficult, students can use a larger ball to bounce by hand.

For Gifted Learners

This lesson may be expanded by having gifted learners develop five additional rate problems for the class to solve.

Home/School Connection

Give students the following assignment to complete at home:

> Jog outdoors or on a treadmill for 5 minutes. Stop and use a stopwatch to measure the number of your heartbeats for 10 seconds. Now walk on the treadmill or outdoors for 5 minutes, and record the number of your heartbeats for 10 seconds. Convert your heart rate measurements into beats per minute. Research healthy heart rates for your age group, and compare them to your own data. Make a graph of your heart rate, and bring it to class with an explanation.

How to Evaluate This Lesson

If you videotaped the gym activity, students may want to watch this as a fun review.

Have the students use the rates that they collected during the basketball and jumping rope activity to solve the following three word problems:

1. To win a contest at a local radio station, you must make 600 baskets in 1 hour. Based on your per-minute rate, how many baskets would you predict you could make in an hour?

2. The school record for jumping rope is 450 jumps in 15 minutes. How many jumps could you do in 15 minutes?

3. Your dad tells you the more baskets you shoot, the more you'll make. How many baskets could you attempt in 27 minutes?

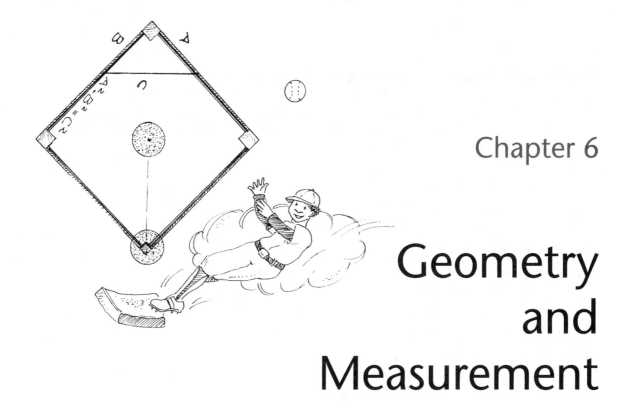

Chapter 6

Geometry
and
Measurement

This chapter is designed to aid teachers in presenting information on geometry in a multitude of ways in order to address many students' learning styles and strengths. Goals include gaining student understanding of lines, angles, and shapes, as well as mastery using formulas such as the Pythagorean theorem, area, and perimeter.

Activity 1: Types of Lines and Angles

Purpose: To understand and identify various types of lines and angles.

Read through the lesson and the adaptations, and make sure you have the supplies you'll need.

For the Main Lesson

chalkboard, overhead projector, computer with presentation software, or interactive whiteboard

lined paper

pencils

protractors (1 for each student)

rulers (1 for each student)

graph paper

For the Adaptations

colored pencils

colored paper

modeling clay

paint stick

colored chalk

masking tape

light-up board with colored pieces

computer with a drawing or painting program

origami paper

stickers

Lesson

1. Pass out the lined paper and protractors.

2. To begin the lesson, you might say something like: "Today we are going to explore various types of lines and angles."

3. Write the following definitions on the board, and ask students to copy the definitions onto their lined paper.

Parallel lines. Lines in a plane that are the same distance apart at all points.

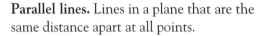

Perpendicular lines. Lines that intersect, forming right angles.

Ray. Part of a line that starts at a given point and goes off in a certain direction forever.

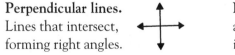

Angle. An angle is formed by the intersection of two rays with a common endpoint. Angles are measured in degrees using a tool called a protractor. An angle may look like any of the following:

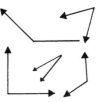

Acute angle. An angle that measures less than 90 degrees.

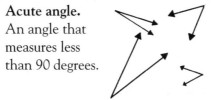

Right angle. An angle that measures exactly ninety degrees.

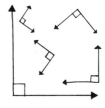

Obtuse angle. An angle that measures more than 90 degrees but less than 180 degrees.

Straight angle. Any angle that measures exactly 180 degrees.

4. Explain that in addition to the different types of angles, there are a few special relationships between pairs of angles. Write the following definitions on the board, and ask students to copy the definitions onto their lined paper:

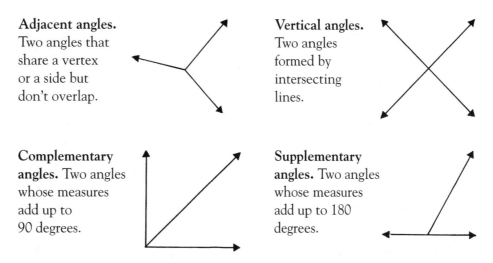

Adjacent angles. Two angles that share a vertex or a side but don't overlap.

Vertical angles. Two angles formed by intersecting lines.

Complementary angles. Two angles whose measures add up to 90 degrees.

Supplementary angles. Two angles whose measures add up to 180 degrees.

5. Show students how to draw these angles and angle pairs by using the protractor and a ruler. The paraprofessional can walk around the room and assist any students who are having difficulties making the different types of angles.

Hand out the Lines and Angles Worksheet, and proceed to work with small groups of students on some of the adaptations.

Lines and Angles Worksheet

Write the definition in the blank provided. Then draw an example of each angle or pair of angles on graph paper using a protractor and a ruler.

1. A right angle _____

_____

2. An acute angle _____

_____

3. Supplementary angles _____

_____

4. An obtuse angle _____

_____

5. Complementary angles _____

_____

6. Vertical angles _____

_____

7. Parallel lines _____

_____

8. Perpendicular lines _____

_____

How to Adapt This Lesson for the Inclusive Classroom

For Learning Disabled Students

Using the definitions presented in class, protractors, and the worksheet, review and reteach this lesson with a small group of students who are struggling with this concept. Strategies such as color-coding angles with colored pencils or highlighters may work to reinforce angle types. For students who continue to struggle with the concept of angles, try the following two strategies that work well to give students visual examples for angles.

1. Make a sundial by sticking a paint stick into a ball of modeling clay so that the clay can be used as a base. Bring the small group outside the building on a sunny day at varying times, each time marking the shadow angles on a sidewalk or playground with colored chalk. Have students identify the angles during different times of the day.

2. Have a small group open and close a classroom door, and identify several angles: for example, a shut door, a door open just a crack, a door that is wide open. Have students mark the angles on the floor with masking tape and then measure them with a protractor.

For Resistant Learners and Students with ADD/ADHD

If the students understand the basic concept of angles, work with them to complete the worksheet, and use a light-up board game as a reward for accurate completion. Here students can reinforce definitions learned by building angles on the light-up board. This will serve as a review and keep students actively engaged in the activity. Computer games also help to retain focus for these students. Show them how to use a drawing and painting program (provided in most computers) to draw and color angles; then have them identify each angle created. Provide immediate positive feedback when they build angles correctly. For extreme focusing difficulties, use points or stickers as a reward after successful completion of each item.

For Students with Physical Disabilities

For students with visual impairments, the light up board may be an effective tool to review all angle definitions.

For Gifted Learners

You can expand this lesson by having students do origami (paper folding). Students can go to the library in pairs and research a few simple origami designs, practice making the designs, and bring the directions and their completed designs back to class. They could then teach the class how to make these items.

Home/School Connection

Give students the following assignment to complete at home:

> Using colored paper and a protractor, have a night of family fun making a mosaic. Cut examples of all the types of angles, with each type of angle in a specific color. Glue the pieces onto an 8½ by 11-inch piece of poster board to make an interesting design. Make a key of the various angles used and colors chosen, and bring your creation to class.

How to Evaluate This Lesson

The lesson on lines and angles is assessed best by using a rubric to determine what the students have mastered and where they need additional instruction. The purpose of the rubric is to assess students' mastery of all definitions of types of angles. Make sure students can identify all angles both by written definition and diagram. Mastery of both categories should be a minimum of 80 percent before students go on to learn higher-level concepts.

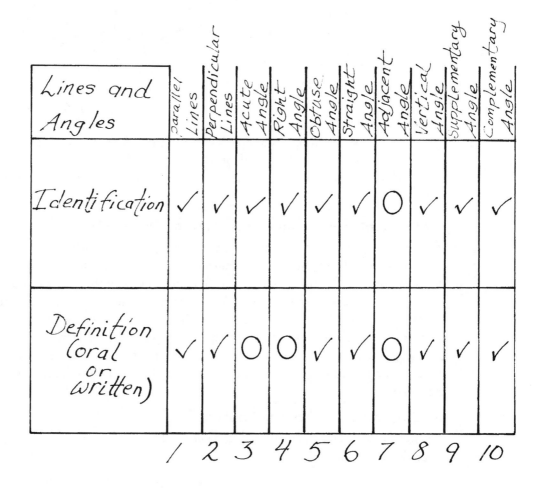

Lines and Angles	Parallel Lines	Perpendicular Lines	Acute Angle	Right Angle	Obtuse Angle	Straight Angle	Adjacent Angle	Vertical Angle	Supplementary Angle	Complementary Angle
Identification	✓	✓	✓	✓	✓	✓	O	✓	✓	✓
Definition (oral or written)	✓	✓	O	O	✓	✓	O	✓	✓	✓
	1	2	3	4	5	6	7	8	9	10

Activity 2: Basic Geometric Shapes

Purpose: To name and define some of the basic shapes used in geometry.

Read through the lesson and the adaptations, and make sure you have the supplies you'll need.

For the Main Lesson

chalkboard, overhead projector, computer with presentation software, or interactive whiteboard

lined paper

dotted paper

rulers

protractors

For the Adaptations

colored markers and/or pencils

index cards

colored foam board

scissors

lunch-sized paper bags

egg timer

Lesson

1. Pass out the lined paper.
2. To begin the lesson, you might say something like: "Today we are going to learn about, identify, and work with the most commonly used shapes in geometry."
3. Write the following Shapes Chart on the board and ask students to copy the chart onto their lined paper. After the lesson, they can keep this sheet in their notebooks for later reference.

Shapes Chart

	Number Sides	Number Corners	Unique Features
Square	4	4	All sides equal, all right angles
Rectangle	4	4	Two pairs of equal parallel sides
Triangle	3	3	
Circle	0	0	Points equidistant from the center
Oval	0	0	Elliptical
Pentagon	5	5	
Hexagon	6	6	
Octagon	8	8	
Parallelogram	4	4	Opposite sides parallel and equal
Rhombus	4	4	Opposite sides parallel and all sides equal
Kite	4	4	Two pairs of consecutive equal sides
Trapezoid	4	4	One pair of opposite sides is parallel

4. Review each geometric shape on the chart; show an example on the board, and explain each shape's unique properties.

Hand out the Basic Geometric Shapes Worksheet, and proceed to work with small groups of students on some of the adaptations.

Name: _____   Date: _____

Basic Geometric Shapes Worksheet

Using dotted paper, rulers, and protractors, draw and label the following shapes. Write the most common characteristic of the shape on the lines provided on the worksheet.

1. Trapezoid _____

   _____

2. Square _____

   _____

3. Rectangle _____

   _____

4. Triangle _____

   _____

5. Parallelogram _____

   _____

6. Hexagon _____

   _____

7. Octagon _____

   _____

8. Pentagon _____

   _____

Attach your diagrams to this worksheet when completed.

How to Adapt This Lesson for the Inclusive Classroom

For Learning Disabled Students

Review and reteach the lesson with a small group of students who are having difficulties remembering basic shapes using the notes taken in class and the worksheet. An effective strategy for this group is playing a basic memory game using color-coded shapes.

Shape Memory Game

1. Each student picks a color for each shape from the shape chart and draws and colors each shape on an index card. They use the same color to write the name of the shape on an additional card.

2. Students give the teacher the cards with the names on them.

3. The teacher shuffles all of the cards together and lays them face down on the table.

4. The teacher briefly turns over the face-down cards so the group can study the items and then puts them back in their place.

5. Students take turns around the table, attempting to match a shape in their hands with the correct concealed card. The student who matches all of his or her cards first is the winner.

For Resistant Learners and Students with ADD/ADHD

If students in this group are struggling remembering shapes, they could review the adapted lesson with the students with learning disabilities. Students who have completed or understand the worksheet can play Geometry Memory and test their creative skills. This game has a great potential to be successful with students who have difficulties focusing and attending to task because the task is short and the boundaries provided by the egg timer are clear.

Geometry Memory

1. Before the class, prepare at least three bags of foam board shapes. For each bag, cut two examples of each shape taught in class.

2. Give each pair of students a piece of white paper and a bag of shapes.

3. Turn over the egg timer, giving one student in the pair 3 minutes to come up with as many designs as he or she can on the white paper using three chosen shapes. For example, you might say, "Make as many designs as you can using circles, rectangles, and squares."

4. While the first student in the pair is designing shapes, the second student should record the shapes used.

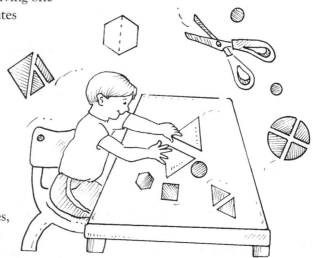

Differentiated Instruction for the Middle School Math Teacher

5. Once this round is completed, the pair change roles and go again. The challenge is to see how many designs they can make out of the shapes.

For Gifted Learners

This lesson may be expanded by having gifted learners participate as a group in making a kaleidoscope or a geodome, which is a domed structure formed by interlocking polygons. Before building, have students go to the library and find books or look on the Internet to find out more about these projects and how to make them.

Home/School Connection

Give students the following assignment to complete at home:

Make a list of items in your house that correspond with the basic shapes covered in class. Find at least two examples of each shape, and bring your list into class to discuss.

How to Evaluate This Lesson

Use a project-centered evaluation. Give students geoboards or dot paper and have them create the following shapes:

Square	Triangle
Rectangle	Pentagon
Parallelogram	Hexagon
Rhombus	Octagon
Trapezoid	

Activity 3: Triangles and the Pythagorean Theorem

Purpose: To understand the different types of triangles and introduce the Pythagorean theorem.

Read through the lesson and the adaptations, and make sure you have the supplies you'll need.

For the Main Lesson

chalkboard, overhead projector, computer with presentation software, or interactive whiteboard

lined paper

For the Adaptations

protractors

colored pencils

rulers

scissors

construction paper

watch with second hand

foam board

calculators

large-faced calculators

Lesson

1. Pass out the lined paper.

2. To begin the lesson, you might say something like: "We have reviewed several shapes in the prior lessons. Today we are going to expand on this concept and examine distinctions among various triangles. We will also examine the Pythagorean theorem, which applies to a specific type of triangle called a right triangle."

3. Write the following definitions on the board, and ask students to copy the definitions onto their lined paper.

Right triangle. A triangle with one right (90 degree) angle.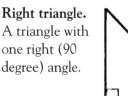

Equilateral triangle: A triangle with three equal sides.

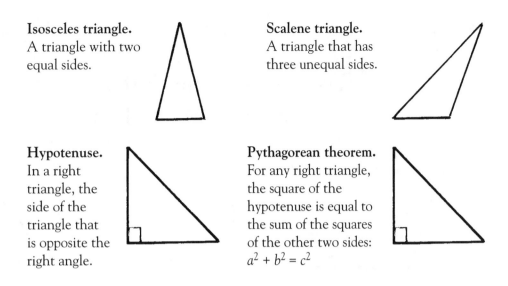

Isosceles triangle.
A triangle with two equal sides.

Scalene triangle.
A triangle that has three unequal sides.

Hypotenuse.
In a right triangle, the side of the triangle that is opposite the right angle.

Pythagorean theorem.
For any right triangle, the square of the hypotenuse is equal to the sum of the squares of the other two sides: $a^2 + b^2 = c^2$

4. Show students how to use the Pythagorean theorem to find the length of the hypotenuse. For example, if a right triangle has one 8-foot leg and one 12-foot leg, what is the length of the hypotenuse?

a. Write the Pythagorean theorem.

$c^2 = a^2 + b^2$

b. Substitute 12 for a and 8 for b.

$c^2 = 12^2 + 8^2$

c. Simplify the equation.

$c^2 = 208$

d. Use a calculator to find the square root of 208.

$c = 14.4$

Hand out the Triangles and the Pythagorean Theorem Worksheet, and proceed to work with small groups of students on some of the adaptations.

Triangles and the Pythagorean Theorem Worksheet

1. Identify the following types of triangles.

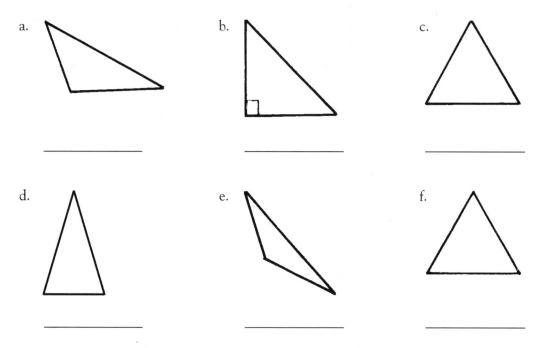

a. _____

b. _____

c. _____

d. _____

e. _____

f. _____

2. Using the Pythagorean theorem, calculate the length of the hypotenuse when the following legs of a right triangle have the measurements shown. Show all work on a separate piece of paper.

a.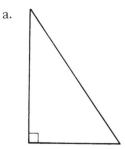

b.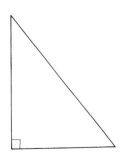

c.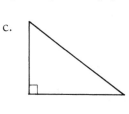

a. _____
(legs: 5 cm, 7 cm)

b. _____
(legs 8 cm, 10 cm)

c. _____
(legs 4 cm, 5 cm)

How to Adapt This Lesson for the Inclusive Classroom

For Learning Disabled Students

Students who struggle with remembering the different types of triangles can be asked to name types of triangles that they see in the classroom. Students can then measure the angles with a protractor or ruler to see if the definitions apply and make a list of the shapes they found.

Students who have difficulties with the complexities of the Pythagorean theorem may benefit from the following strategy.

Step 1: Reteach. Use notes from class, and teach the theory over again using easier problems.

Step 2: Review. Review the steps, and informally assess the student's knowledge. Clarification, visualization, modeling, and repetition are all parts of this step. Do not proceed until the student has an understanding of the problem.

Step 3: Reinforce. Reinforce the concepts learned by having students model how to solve a new problem that you have designed. Do not proceed until this step is mastered.

Step 4: Slowly increase the difficulty of the problems. Incorporate all techniques from steps 1 to 3 until the student gains mastery of the technique.

During the last step, the paraprofessional or teacher will participate less and less, until the student is basically solving the problem aloud by himself or herself. Once the student has successfully mastered and modeled how to solve these problems, he or she can complete the worksheet.

For Resistant Learners and Students with ADD/ADHD

Students with a behavioral disability who are particularly distracted or need consistent discipline during this lesson but appear to understand the basic concepts may benefit from teaming up with another strong student and completing the worksheet in pairs. This will keep the students actively engaged.

Students who have memory issues can play a game called Name That Shape with a bag of shapes and a watch with a second hand.

Name That Shape

1. Make several types of triangles as well as shapes from previous activities out of foam board.

2. See how many shapes each student in the group can name in 1 minute. Students with the highest scores can obtain points to be exchanged for a homework pass, a snack from the cafeteria, or something else.

For Students with Visual Impairments

Have large-faced calculators to help these students find square roots and solve problems using the Pythagorean theorem.

For Gifted Learners

This lesson may be expanded by having gifted learners work as a team to develop word problems using the Pythagorean theorem that relate to the middle school environment.

This group can present two chosen problems for the class to solve as a whole. Some examples are a baseball diamond, school dismissal patterns, and a tennis court.

Home/School Connection

Give students the following assignments to complete at home:

> If it's a nice day, set up a game of baseball, softball, or kickball to play with your family. Mark all bases. Before you play, determine the distance between second base and home by measuring the distances between home plate and first base (one leg of the right triangle) and between first and second base (the other leg of the right triangle) and then using the Pythagorean theorem.
>
> In bad weather, design a "stained glass window" using construction paper and colored cellophane wrap by cutting triangle-shaped holes in the construction paper that include all of the different types of triangles discussed in class. Cover the holes with colored cellophane, and bring the finished project class to hang in the windows.

How to Evaluate This Lesson

For this lesson, we suggest using traditional assessment methods—a graded worksheet, the completed Home/School Connection, and a teacher-made test—to determine how well students remember the different types of triangles and if they have mastered the use of the Pythagorean theorem.

Activity 4: Area and Perimeter of Quadrilaterals and Triangles

Purpose: To be able to calculate the area and perimeter of quadrilaterals and triangles.

Read through the lesson and the adaptations, and make sure you have the supplies you'll need.

For the Main Lesson

chalkboard, overhead projector, computer with presentation software, or interactive whiteboard

lined paper

For the Adaptations

dotted paper

graph paper

rulers

colored highlighters

plastic interlocking building blocks

index cards

sugar cubes

white glue

audiocassettes

large-faced calculators

ingredients for making brownies (see the recipe on p. 130)

egg timer

Lesson

1. Pass out the lined paper.

2. Explain to the students that you will be looking at quadrilaterals, which are four-sided polygons, and ways to measure them. Draw a rectangle and a square on a piece of graph paper on the overhead.

3. Ask the students if they have ever heard of the word *perimeter*, and facilitate a discussion. Then give them a real-life example, such as, "The perimeter of a garden would be equal to the amount of fence it would take to go all the way around it." Then ask for definitions of *perimeter* in the students' own words, and record them on the board.

4. Write the following definition on the board, and ask students to copy it onto their lined paper.

   Perimeter. The distance around a figure; the sum of all sides.

   As an example, a rectangle with a width of 5 feet and a length of 4 feet would have a perimeter of 18 feet: 4 + 5 + 4 + 5 = 18.

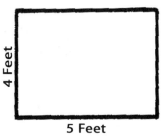

5. Ask the students if they have heard the word *area,* and facilitate a discussion. Then give them a real-life example, such as, "The area of a bathroom floor is equal to the number of 1-foot square tiles it takes to cover the floor." Then ask for definitions of area in the students' own words and record them on the board.

6. Write the following definition on the board, and ask students to copy the definition onto their lined paper.

   Area. A measure of how much surface is covered by a figure.

7. Draw a square on a piece of graph paper on the overhead. Have a student come up to the board to count how many small squares are enclosed by the square. Do a few more examples. Some students may figure out a short-cut to counting the squares: multiplying two sides.

8. Explain that the areas of different figures can be calculated using formulas. Have students write the following formulas on their sheets of paper as you explain them on the board. Discuss why there are different formulas. For instance, a triangle is base times height divided by two because it is half of a square or rectangle.

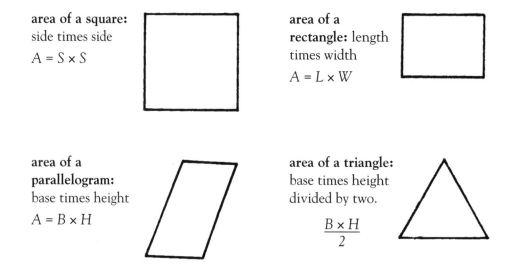

area of a square: side times side

$A = S \times S$

area of a rectangle: length times width

$A = L \times W$

area of a parallelogram: base times height

$A = B \times H$

area of a triangle: base times height divided by two.

$\dfrac{B \times H}{2}$

Hand out the Area and Perimeter of Quadrilaterals and Triangles Worksheet, and proceed to work with small groups of students on some of the adaptations.

Name: _____   Date: _____

Area and Perimeter
of Quadrilaterals and
Triangles Worksheet

1. Find the perimeter of the following shapes. Draw each shape on a separate piece of graph paper so that 1 foot equals one side of a square on the graph paper.

   a. A square with 4-foot sides. _____

   b. A triangle with 4-foot sides and a 3-foot base. _____

   c. A rectangle with a 16-foot width and a 56-foot length. _____

   d. A rectangle with a 25-foot width and an 8-foot length. _____

2. Find the area of the following triangles:

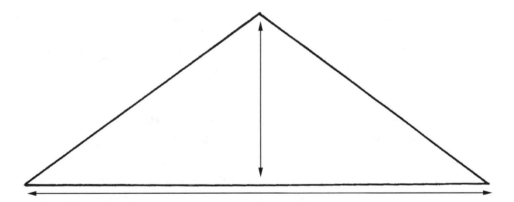

   a. Triangle A: 12-foot base and a 14-foot height. _____

   b. Triangle B: a 14-foot base and an 11-foot height. _____

   c. Triangle C: a 12-foot base and a 9-foot height. _____

3. Find the area of the following quadrilaterals:

   a. A square with 20-foot sides. _____

   b. A rectangle with a 15-foot length and a 4-foot width. _____

   c. A parallelogram a height of 8- and 12-foot sides. _____

   d. A rectangle with a 12-foot length and an 11-foot width. _____

How to Adapt This Lesson for the Inclusive Classroom

For Learning Disabled Students

Review and reteach the lesson with a small group of students who are struggling with this concept using the formulas and notes given in class and the worksheet. Dotted paper and graph paper can be used to make a key for size accuracy when solving items. Different colored highlighters can be used to mark length, width, and height on each shape, and the calculator can be used to calculate and recheck work. You can assign every other item of the worksheet so students do not become overwhelmed by the assignment. For students who still continue to struggle, show them how to build models with interlocking plastic building blocks or sugar cubes to denote area. Count up all the blocks and cubes in the model, and show how that same number can be found using the correct formula. If the students use sugar cubes, they can glue the sculptures together with white glue.

For Students with Physical Disabilities, Perceptual Impairments, or Short-Term Memory Difficulties

Students who have difficulties reading, seeing, or remembering the formulas for areas and perimeters may use a small audiocassette during the teacher's lesson to record this information. They also can use an index card to write down each formula and audiotape. The information then is presented in a multisensory format. A large-faced calculator may also be used to solve equations and check work.

For Gifted Learners

Give students a creative problem of designing a new quad or central meeting place that could include vending machines, a pool table, and other attractions they choose. The space has to be large enough to accommodate the items they select. They can develop a blueprint of the space, including dimensions, overall area, and perimeter, as well as area and perimeter of individual items.

For All Learners

Sometimes the entire class can benefit from a multisensory activity to reinforce a concept while having fun. This activity needs to take place in a room where a water source and stove are readily available.

Divide the students into three cooking groups. Give each group a similar but slightly different-size four-sided disposable pan. Allow students to measure the pan as well as all of the ingredients needed to make brownies as described in the following recipe. Students can calculate the area and perimeter of their pan while they are baking their snack. Once brownies are cooled, cut them into different triangle and quadrilateral shapes. Before they eat them, students can find the area and perimeter of individual brownies.

Rich Brownie Bars

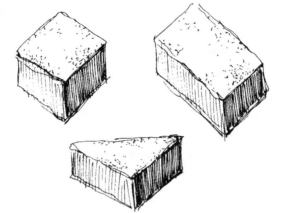

vegetable oil cooking spray

1 cup margarine or butter

4 ounces milk chocolate

2 cups sugar

1½ cups all-purpose flour

4 large eggs

1 teaspoon salt

1 teaspoon baking powder

1 tablespoon vanilla extract

1 cup minichips

1. Preheat the oven to 350°F. (Under adult supervision!)
2. Spray the baking pan with vegetable oil cooking spray.
3. Put the margarine or butter and 4 ounces of chocolate into a saucepan.
4. Cook over medium heat, stirring constantly with the wooden spoon, until the margarine or butter and chocolate melt. Turn off the heat and set aside.
5. In a medium bowl, use another wooden spoon to combine the sugar and flour.
6. In a small bowl, beat the eggs until they are broken up.
7. Add the salt, baking powder, and vanilla extract to the eggs. Whisk together.
8. Add the egg mixture and the melted margarine or butter and chocolate mixture to the flour and stir until well combined, about 50 strokes.
9. Fold in the minichips.
10. Spread the batter into the pan and bake for approximately 30 to 35 minutes, or until a wooden pick inserted into the center comes out clean.
11. Cool the brownies before cutting.

Home/School Connection

Give students the following assignment to complete at home:

Have a family member help you with an imaginary room makeover. As part of the planning, measure the size of your room and figure out how much carpet you need to cover the floor and how much wallpaper you need to cover the walls. Go to a store, and look at swatches of the carpet and wallpaper you like best, and determine what it would cost to use these in your room. Draw a sketch of your redecorated room on poster board. Attach your swatches, if you have any, and include all costs. Bring all information to class to present and discuss.

How to Evaluate This Lesson

For this lesson, we recommend evaluating student understanding using a game format. Divide the class into four small groups by skill level and abilities. You will also need the problems from the worksheet, some additional teacher-created problems that use all of the formulas in the lesson, an egg timer, two or three calculators for each small group, and lined paper for each student. Here is how to play the game:

1. Write a formula on the board for each group, and give each group a problem. Then turn over the egg timer.

2. Each group jointly solves its problem.

3. When time is up, one person from each group gives the group answer. If the answer is correct, 1 point is awarded to that team. Keep score, and repeat this process until you've gone through all the problems. The team with the highest points is the winner.

When evaluating students' understanding using a game, take mental notes on students' behaviors. Make sure one student does not dominate the group, and all are contributing to the work presented.

Activity 5: Properties of Circles

Purpose: To define and understand the properties of circles and how they relate to geometry.
Read through the lesson and the adaptations, and make sure you have the supplies you'll need.

For the Main Lesson

chalkboard, overhead projector, computer with presentation software, or interactive whiteboard

lined paper

calculators

For the Adaptations

large-faced calculators

assorted lids from coffee cans or plastic containers

scissors

rulers

colored highlighters

compasses

construction paper

2 or 3 paper towel rolls

1 skein yarn

several pairs of small scissors

index cards

Lesson

1. Pass out the lined paper and calculators. Explain to students that you are going to discuss the properties of circles, and ask students to brainstorm what they know about circles. Write their responses on the board.

2. Write the following definitions and formulas on the board, and ask students to copy them on their index cards.

   Radius. The distance from anywhere on the edge of a circle to its center is the circle's radius. The radius, or *r*, is always half the diameter of the circle.

   The formula is: Radius = diameter ÷ 2.

   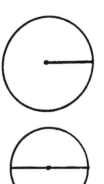

   Diameter. A line segment that passes through the center of the circle and has both endpoints on the circle. The diameter cuts the circle exactly in half.

   The formula is: Diameter = Radius × 2.

Circumference. The distance around a circle.

The formula is: Circumference = π × diameter. The Greek symbol π, pi, describes the ratio of the circumference to the diameter of a circle (C ÷ d); it equals about 3.14.

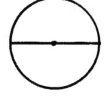

Area: The area of a circle is also calculated using pi. The area of a circle is the amount of space inside a circle. The area of a circle is equal to pi times the radius squared.

The formula is: Area = πr^2

3. Give students some measurements for parts of circles, and have them practice calculating—for example, the diameter given the radius or the circumference given the diameter.

Hand out the Properties of Circles Worksheet, and proceed to work with small groups of students on some of the adaptations.

Properties of Circles Worksheet

1. Define the following terms in your own words:

   a. radius _____

   _____

   _____

   b. diameter _____

   _____

   _____

   c. circumference _____

   _____

   _____

   d. area _____

   _____

   _____

2. Solve the following problems:

   a. Find the circumference of a circle whose diameter is 9 feet. _____

   b. Find the radius of a circle whose diameter is 10 feet. _____

   c. Find the area of a circle whose diameter is 6 feet. _____

   d. Find the diameter of a circle whose radius is 6 feet. _____

How to Adapt This Lesson for the Inclusive Classroom

For Learning Disabled Students

Review and reteach this lesson with a small group of students who are struggling with this concept, using the formulas and notes given in class and the worksheet. Students can find the radius, diameter, area, and circumference of circles by using various sizes of containers and lids. Parts of a circle can be marked with colored highlighters to create a visual example of items on the worksheet. Calculations can be worked through on the calculator. Circles can also be drawn and expanded by working with a compass.

Yarn can be used to measure the diameter of circles. Since the circumference is roughly three times the diameter, students can measure the diameter three times and cut a larger piece of yarn to illustrate this concept. Again, large-faced calculators should be available to aid students with visual or perceptual impairments when calculating data.

For students who continue to struggle with this concept, there are some books that can be helpful, such as Cindy Neuschwander's *Sir Cumference and the First Round Table* (2002) and *Sir Cumference and the Dragon of Pi* (2002).

Resistant Learners and Students with ADD/ADHD

If a student with behavioral difficulties understands the concepts presented on the worksheet but has a difficult time focusing, allow this student to work with a buddy. This will keep the learning interactive. Check on the pair to make sure both parties are working, and guide this practice if need be.

For the Gifted Learner

This lesson may be expanded on by having gifted learners develop a scaled model drawing of a sand castle or snowman. They can experiment with various circle sizes and calculate the scaled and projected size of the item. A further group activity could be to make an actual sand castle or snowman to demonstrate this, time and materials permitting.

Home/School Connection

Give students the following assignment to complete at home:

> Make a list of ten round items that you can find in your kitchen; for example, plates, cereal bowls, measuring cups, and paper towel rolls. Find the circumference, area, diameter and radius of these items, and list from smallest to largest on a piece of poster board. Bring your poster to class.

How to Evaluate This Lesson

Use a group activity of pizza measurement. Assess the students on how well they understand the concepts presented in class and their work as a group.

Supplies Needed

3 uncut pizzas ordered from a local pizzeria

3 pizza cutters

paper plates

napkins

index cards

3 rulers or cloth tape measures

calculators

Directions

1. Wash hands thoroughly.
2. Divide the class into three groups based on skill level.
3. Give each group an index card and one of the pizzas.
4. Ask each group to measure and calculate the radius, diameter, circumference, and area of their pizza.
5. The students should write the measurement or the appropriate formula on their note cards and show the calculations they used to get their answer.
6. When everyone has completed the activity, cut up the pizzas and enjoy!

Activity 6: Polyhedrons

Purpose: To understand the features and different types of polyhedrons.

Read through the lesson and the adaptations, and make sure you have the supplies you'll need.

For the Main Lesson

chalkboard, overhead projector, computer with presentation software, or interactive whiteboard

lined paper

graph paper

manila folders

construction paper

colored markers

clear tape

white glue

rulers

scissors

For the Adaptations

plastic straws

gumdrops or modeling clay

Lesson

1. Pass out the lined paper.
2. Write the following definitions on the board, and ask students to copy the definitions on their lined paper.

   Polygon. A figure such as a triangle or quadrilateral whose sides are line segments.

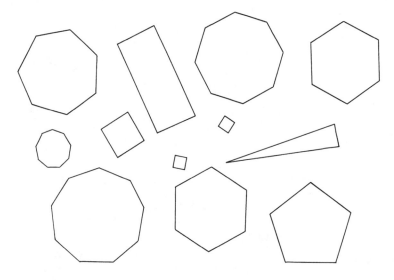

Polyhedron. A solid (three-dimensional) figure that has polygons as its faces.

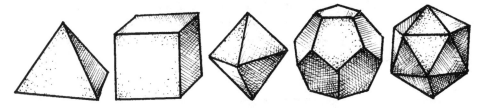

Prism. A polyhedron with two congruent (the same) and parallel faces.

Pyramid. A polyhedron in which the base is a polygon and the other faces are triangles. The triangles share a common vertex.

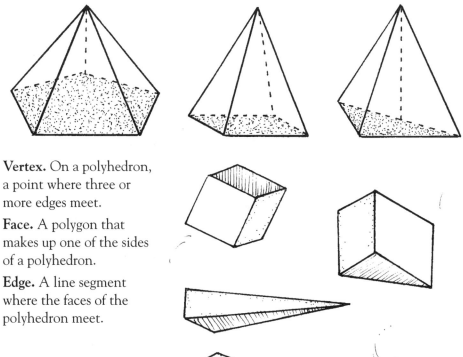

Vertex. On a polyhedron, a point where three or more edges meet.

Face. A polygon that makes up one of the sides of a polyhedron.

Edge. A line segment where the faces of the polyhedron meet.

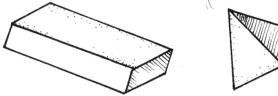

3. Say each definition, and draw an example of each on the board.

4. Explain that polyhedrons are named based on the number of faces they have. For example, a triangular pyramid has four sides and is a tetrahedron. A triangular prism and a rectangular pyramid have five sides and are called pentahedrons. A rectangular prism with six sides is called a hexahedron. And a polyhedron with eight sides is called an octahedron.

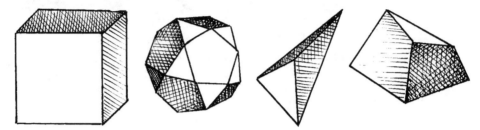

Hand out the Polyhedrons Worksheet, and proceed to work with small groups of students on some of the adaptations. Also hand out the worksheet packet, and explain to the students that they are going to be making models of polyhedrons in class.

Polyhedrons Worksheet

1. In your own words, define the following terms:

   a. pyramid _____

   _____

   b. prism _____

   _____

   c. face _____

   _____

   d. polyhedron _____

   _____

   e. edge _____

   _____

   f. vertex _____

   _____

2. Using the flat patterns (also called nets) in the Polyhedrons Worksheet Packet, make the following polyhedron models and fill in the chart below.

	Rectangular Prism	Triangular Pyramid	Octahedron	Triangular Prism	Cube
Faces					
Vertices					
Edges					

Polyhedrons Worksheet Packet

Rectangular prism

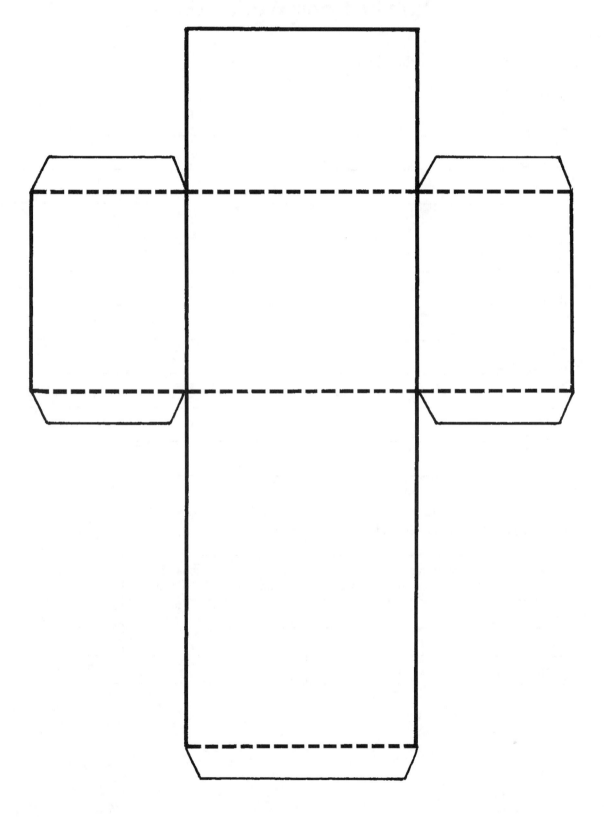

Triangular pyramid

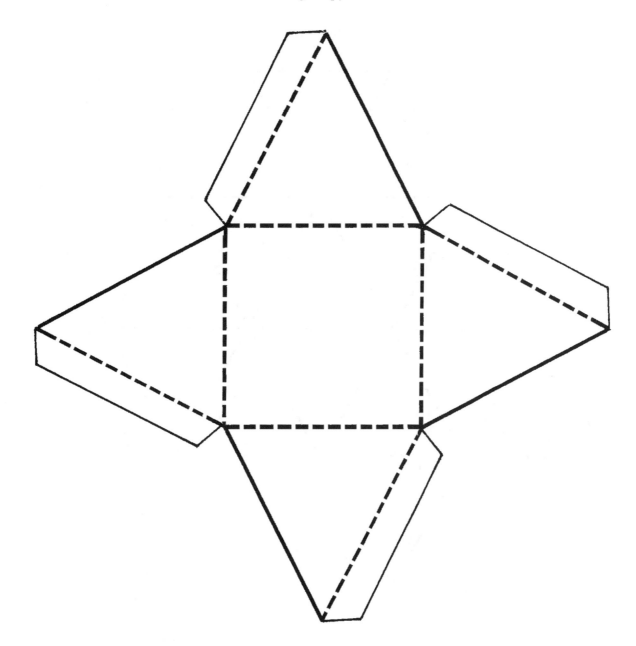

Octahedron

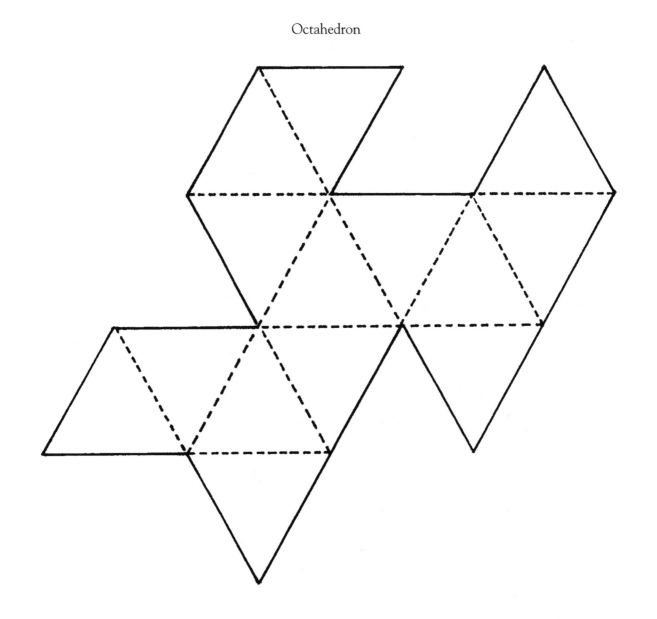

Triangular prism

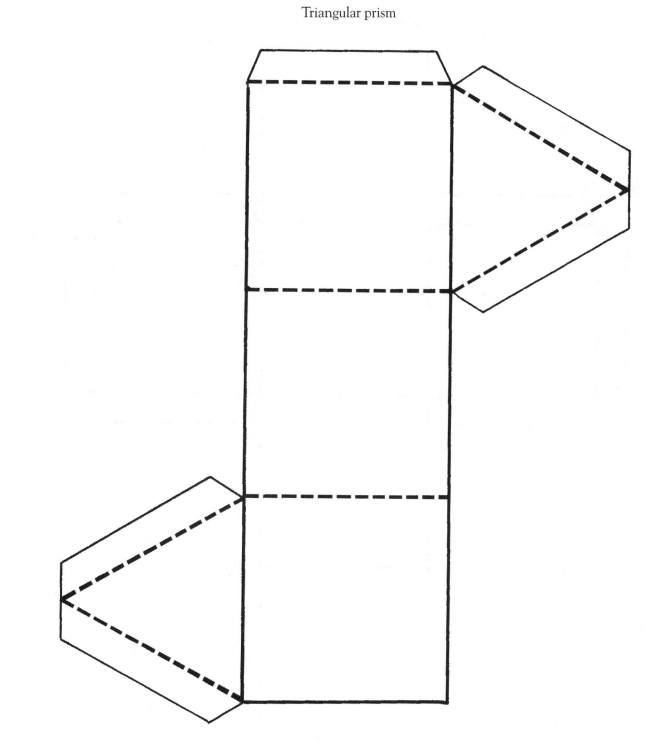

Cube

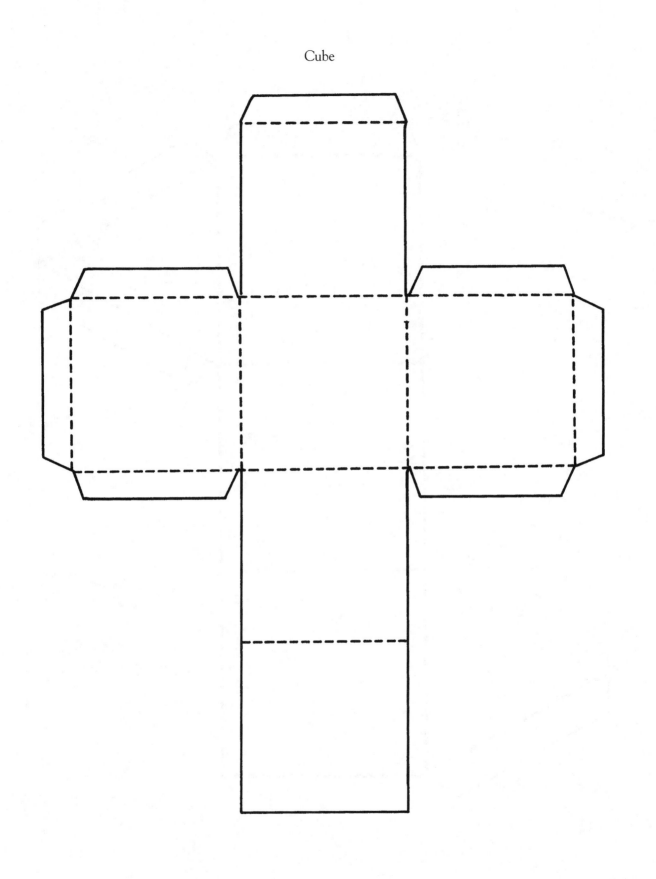

How to Adapt This Lesson for the Inclusive Classroom

For Learning Disabled Students

Review and reteach the lesson in a small group setting with students who are struggling with this concept, using the notes taken in class and the worksheet. Show students how to make the five basic polyhedron designs that are included on the chart on the Polyhedrons Worksheet. Once they have mastered the method of construction on one item, have the students repeat the process until they have made all of the shapes in the packet. Work with the students to fill out the data on faces, edges, and vertices. Students may work together to help each other. Data in the chart may be color-coded, such as using a different color for each polyhedron, to aid in memory.

For Resistant Learners or Students with ADD/ADHD or Short-Term Memory Difficulties

Working side-by-side with these students and using the script below can aid in focusing, memory, and understanding when completing the worksheet tasks.

Polyhedrons Worksheet Script

1. "Here are the pattern and instructions needed to make a cube. The first step is to cut out the design on all solid lines and fold along the dotted lines." The student then verbalizes and models this script and completes step 1.

2. "Next I will put my shape together to make sure it looks like a cube. When all sides are together, I will tape the shape together with clear tape." The student verbalizes and models this script and completes step 2.

3. "Now, I will complete my chart. To find the faces, I will count all the sides that make up the cube. I count one-two-three-four-five-six sides or faces of the cube. I'll write this number on my chart." The student verbalizes and models this script and completes step 3.

4. "Next, I will count the places where faces of the line segments meet. These are the edges. Let's count together: one, two, three, four, five, six, seven, eight, nine, ten, eleven, and twelve. There are twelve edges on this cube. I'll write this number on my chart." The student verbalizes and models this script and completes step 4.

5. "Finally, I will count the points where the edges meet. These are called the vertices. I count one, two, three, four, five, six, seven, eight points here. There are eight vertices on this cube. I'll write this number on my chart. The student verbalizes and models this script and completes the final step.

This process can be repeated with the other polyhedrons on the chart. (*Note:* Other polyhedra models can be obtained and printed from www.korthalsaltes.com.indes.html.)

For Students with Physical Disabilities

This lesson may be a struggle for students with neurological difficulties, fine motor control, or visual impairments, because folding and taping can be an intricate task. A simple way to make this easier is to enlarge all shapes in the worksheet packet on a printer. Using plastic straws and gumdrops or clay to build polyhedron shapes can be an interesting, fun alternative for these students. The straws can represent all of the lines on the net diagram, and the gumdrops can be used to join all straws to make the polyhedron. Complete the faces first; then connect the straws to each other through the gumdrops.

For Gifted Learners

These students may design a polyhedron to represent the packaging for an item. Students must come up with sound reasoning for their package choice, a label, a way to open the box, and a product name. The model must be at least three times the size as the net diagrams in the worksheet packet. Students can use materials such as manila folders, construction paper, colored markers, clear tape, white glue, rulers, and scissors to complete their package. They may work collaboratively or in pairs. All packaging items can be placed on display in the classroom.

Home/School Connection

Give students the following assignment to complete at home:

> With your family, find at least ten examples of polyhedrons in your house. Make a chart similar to the one on the worksheet, and give the number of faces, vertices, and edges in each item.

How to Evaluate this Lesson

For this lesson we recommend using a student-teacher interview and traditional test grade to determine mastery of polyhedrons. The teacher-made test should include definitions of polyhedrons and related terms, identification of basic shapes, and calculations of the number of vertices, edges, and faces for each polyhedron.

Activity 7: Surface Area of Prisms

Purpose: To find the surface area of prisms.

Read through the lesson and the adaptations, and make sure you have the supplies you'll need.

For the Main Lesson

chalkboard, overhead projector, computer with presentation software, or interactive whiteboard

lined paper

centimeter squared paper

For the Adaptations

poster-size graph paper

polysterene plastic shapes of rectangles, trapezoids, and squares (available at most craft stores)

shoe boxes, jewelry boxes, juice boxes

calculators

large-faced calculator

3 or 4 cloth tape measures

colored pencils

Lesson

1. Pass out the lined paper and centimeter squared paper.

2. Draw a cube, and write the definition of *surface area* on the board. Read the definition aloud, and ask the students to copy it down on their lined paper.

   Surface area of a polyhedron. The sum of the areas of all its faces.

3. Ask the students to draw a 4-centimeter cube on their centimeter squared paper.

4. Explain the formula needed to find the surface area of the cube: "To find the surface area, you need to find the area of each face. Then find the sum of all the faces. The cube has six faces. To find the area of each face, multiply the length times the width, which for a cube means squaring any side. To find the surface area, multiply the number of faces by the area of each face."

   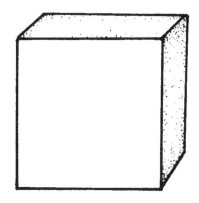

   The surface area of a cube = $6a^2$, where a is the length of any side of the cube. The area of one face of the cube in the example equals $4 \times 4 = 16$ square centimeters: $6 \times 16 = 96$. The surface area of the cube is 96 square centimeters.

5. Next explain how to find the surface area of a rectangular prism. A rectangular prism has six sides and at least three pairs of matching sides. So the standard formula for surface area is:

    Surface area of a rectangular prism = $2lw + 2wh + 2lh$, where l equals the length, w equals the width, and h equals the height.

6. Write the following example on the board, and draw the prism.

    Calculate the surface area of a $3 \times 2 \times 5$-inch rectangular prism.

    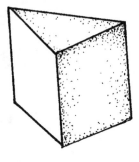

    Then say, "To find the surface area of a rectangle, count up the number of sides that are the same size. In this example, there are two sides that are 3×2 inches, two sides that are 3×5 inches, and two sides that are 2×5 inches. To find the surface area, add the area of all of the sides together."

    Here is the formula for the rectangle in the example:

    $2 \times (3 \times 2) + 2 \times (3 \times 5) + 2 \times (2 \times 5) = 12 + 30 + 20 = 62$ square inches.

Hand out the Surface Area of Prisms Worksheet, and proceed to work with small groups of students on some of the adaptations.

Differentiated Instruction for the Middle School Math Teacher

Name: _____ Date: _____

Surface Area of Prisms Worksheet

Find the surface area of each prism, and write it on the prism.

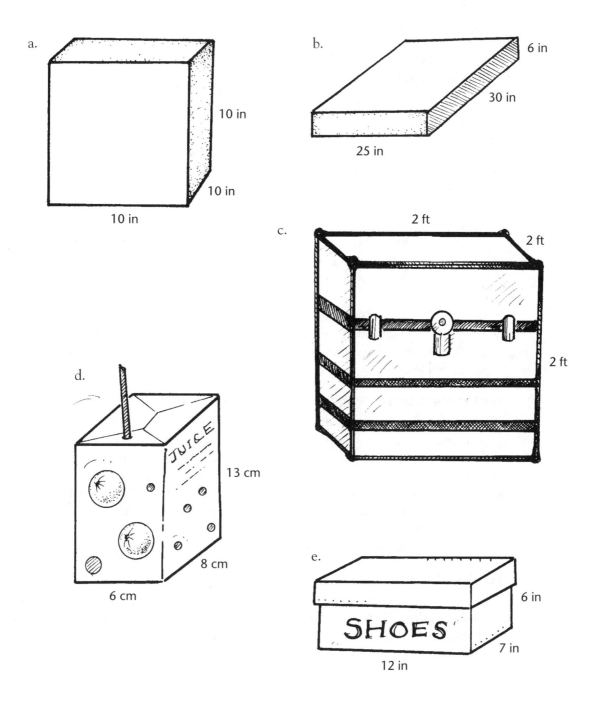

a. 10 in, 10 in, 10 in

b. 6 in, 30 in, 25 in

c. 2 ft, 2 ft, 2 ft

d. 13 cm, 8 cm, 6 cm

e. 6 in, 7 in, 12 in

How to Adapt This Lesson for the Inclusive Classroom

For Learning Disabled Students

Review and reteach the lesson with a small group of students who are struggling with this concept, using the notes taken in class and the worksheet. Students can use different real objects to find the surface areas of different types of prisms. Length and width of prisms can also be color-coded, such as lengths being blue and widths being yellow, to aid in organization of the formulas. Students may use these strategies in conjunction with or separate from the worksheet to reinforce their understanding of this concept. All work should be checked with calculators.

For Students with Physical and Perceptual Disabilities

This lesson may be taught using poster-sized graph paper to help students make a scaled diagram of prisms. The visual aid will help students to remember the information, and have a visual representation while calculating the surface area.

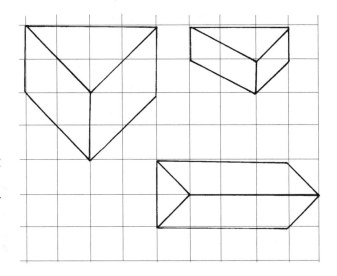

Students with visual impairments may benefit from finding the surface area of various large manipulatives, such as polysterene plastic shapes of cubes and rectangles and different types of boxes: shoe boxes, small costume jewelry boxes, juice boxes, and others. A large-faced calculator can help students more easily calculate surface area problems.

For Resistant Learners and Students with ADD/ADHD

If a student with a behavioral disability is having difficulty focusing but understands the concept of surface area and prisms, pair him or her with another student who understands the formulas, and have them alternate the completion of items on the worksheet. Students can check each other's work with the calculator before handing the assignment in, so that both parties will get exposure to all items. This will keep the learning somewhat brief and interactive, and keep both parties actively engaged. Provide immediate and frequent forms of positive feedback for a job well done. If students finish the work effectively, generate some more problems to be accomplished in the same way for the pair.

For Gifted Learners

This lesson may be expanded by having gifted learners develop surface area problems that are relevant to the middle school environment. Ideas include finding surface areas of logos on T-shirts, desktops, book cases, CDs, and DVDs. Problems can be presented to the class to solve as a group at the end of the activity.

Home/School Connection

Give students the following assignment to complete at home:

> Find some boxes, wrapping paper, and fun items from around the house that would make good gag gifts to exchange with your family. Calculate the surface area of the boxes you are wrapping and estimate how much wrapping paper you will need to wrap the gifts. Bring your findings and calculations to class, along with a description of your present exchange.

How to Evaluate This Lesson

We recommend evaluating the lesson on surface area of prisms using a review game, Serving Up Surface Area, to determine mastery of this concept.

Serving Up Surface Area

1. Form students into four teams. Each team chooses a spokesperson.
2. Give each student a piece of lined paper and a calculator.
3. Put the dimensions of a prism on the board, and ask each team to determine the surface area of the figure. Students work individually at first and then consult with their teammates.
4. The spokesperson for each group gives the group's answer. One point is awarded for a correct answer.
5. Make the problems increasingly difficult as the game progresses. Points are awarded at the end of each round.
6. The team with the most points at the end of the game wins.

Chapter 7

Data Analysis and Probability

This chapter is designed to aid teachers in presenting information on analyzing data and probability in a multitude of ways in order to address many students' learning styles and strengths. The goals are gaining student understanding of measures of central tendency, learning how to read and construct different types of graphs, and learning about probability.

Activity 1: Finding the Mean

Purpose: To calculate the mean as a measure of central tendency.

Read through the lesson and the adaptations, and make sure you have the supplies you'll need.

For the Main Lesson

chalkboard, overhead projector, computer with presentation software, or interactive whiteboard

lined paper

For the Adaptations

index cards

manila folders

colored markers

highlighters

colored pencils

calculators

Lesson

1. Pass out the lined paper.

2. Explain to students that you will be looking at one way to measure what is called the *central tendency*, which is where the middle of the data is. Write the following definition on the board, and ask students to copy it onto their paper:

   Mean. The mathematical average you obtain from a set of numbers.

3. Once the students have finished copying the definition, you might say something like: "Let's work through an example of mean on a set of numbers that represents a student's test and quiz grades for one marking period in social studies."

4. Write the following numbers on the board:

   80, 85, 90, 95, 100

   Then say, "To find the mean, add up all of the test scores."

   80 + 85 + 90 + 95 + 100 = 450

   "Then divide by the number of test scores to find the mean, or average, test score for the marking period."

   450 ÷ 5 = 90

   "Ninety is the mean, or average, test score for that period in social studies."

   Hand out the Finding the Mean Worksheet, and proceed to work with small groups of students on some of the adaptations.

Finding the Mean Worksheet

Find the mean for the following problems. Show all work, and check your answers with a calculator.

1. Find the mean price of a bouquet of flowers at a farmer's market:

    $3, $4, $2, $5, $3, $6, $3

    _____

2. Find the mean number of pages in a set of books:

    234,   333,   198,   222,   253,   219,   244,   266,   195

    _____

3. Find the mean temperature for San Francisco, California, over a 12-day period:

    55°F,   57°F,   63°F,   67°F,   68°F,   68°F,   62°F,   61°F,   69°F,   67°F,   62°F,   60°F

    _____

4. Police radar recorded the following speeds of cars traveling on a town road.
    Calculate the mean speed.

    25 mph,   32 mph,   37 mph,   19 mph,   22 mph,   18 mph

    _____

5. Find the mean amount of time it took John to run the quarter-mile.

    60 seconds,   90 seconds,   72 seconds,   59 seconds,   78 seconds,   68 seconds

    _____

How to Adapt This Lesson for the Inclusive Classroom

For Learning Disabled Students

Review and reteach with a small group of students who are struggling with this concept, using the notes taken in class and the worksheet. Calculators should be used to check and recheck averages to help those who understand the concept but may be having trouble with the arithmetic. For students who continue to struggle with the concept of mean, a classroom poll can be designed and data collected on topics of interest to students, such as the number of CDs or DVDs they own or how many like sushi or pizza. Then students can calculate the mean from these data. Data can be presented on a chart as a visual aid to reinforce concepts learned.

For Resistant Learners and Students with ADD/ADHD

For students with behavioral or attentional difficulties who are struggling with the concept of finding the mean, invite them to join the group of children with learning disabilities. Encouraging them to focus on personal interests will motivate and inspire student interest and should minimize focusing concerns.

For Gifted Learners

This lesson may be expanded by having gifted learners solve more complex problems using the mean. You can show these students how to calculate the sum of a group of items given the mean and the number of items (Sum ÷ items = Mean; for example, in example 1 that follows, $S \div 25 = 80$ so $S = 25 \times 80$, or 2,000). You can design problems for them to work on like the other example:

1. The mean of 25 test scores is 80. What is the sum of these test scores?
2. The mean number of a set of numbers is 54. There are 25 items in the set. What is the sum of the numbers?

Students may be encouraged to develop their own advanced equations.

Home/School Connection

Give students the following assignment to complete at home:

> Calculate the mean number of minutes that all family members watch TV. Record the minutes on an index card, and bring it to class.

How to Evaluate This Lesson

This evaluation has two parts:

Category 1: Conceptual Understanding (70%). This is evaluated by a student-teacher demonstration. Give each student a 3 × 5 note card with the same problem asking them to find the mean of a set of numbers. Give the students time to solve the problem and check their answer with a calculator. When the time is up, call students individually to privately give their answer, explain how they solved the problem, and demonstrate how they got the answer using a calculator.

Category 2: Participation in Class (30%). This is evaluated with a student-teacher interview: Once students finish the conceptual understanding segment of this evaluation, interview each student to mutually determine his or her level of class participation. Students will be given full credit if both teacher and student feel that the student actively participated in both large and small groups.

Activity 2: Finding the Median and Mode

Purpose: To understand and define median and mode.

Read through the lesson and the adaptations, and make sure you have the supplies you'll need.

For the Main Lesson

chalkboard, overhead projector, computer with presentation software, or interactive whiteboard

lined paper

For the Adaptations

graph paper

colored candies

1 set of 2-pound hand weights or 1 hackey sack or "stress ball"

poster board

index cards

4 reusable plastic mats

4 sets of water-soluble markers

egg timer

Lesson

1. Pass out lined and graph paper.

2. Write the following definition on the board, and ask students to copy it on their lined paper:

   Median. The middle number in a set of numbers when the numbers are arranged in numerical order.

3. As an example of how to find the median, take a survey of how many students like five chosen flavors of ice cream. Have students raise their hands when their favorite flavor of ice cream is called and count how many chose that flavor— for example:

Chocolate	7
Vanilla	5
Strawberry	4
Coffee	2
Chocolate mint	9

4. To find the median of these numbers, arrange the data in numerical order:

   2, 4, 5, 7, 9

   The number in the middle, 5, is the median number. The median is the middle number in a sequence.

5. Ask students to copy down this rule about medians:

   If a set has an odd number of numbers, the middle number is the median. If the set has an even number of numbers, the median is the average of the two middle numbers in the set.

6. Now write the following definition on the board and ask students to copy it down on their lined paper:

Mode. The number that occurs most often in a set.

What if you added the teacher and paraprofessionals to the ice cream survey and the numbers came out like this?

Chocolate	7
Vanilla	5
Strawberry	4
Coffee	2
Chocolate mint	4

The mode in this set is 4, because it is the number that occurs the most in the sequence.

Hand out the Median and Mode Worksheet, and proceed to work with small groups of students on some of the adaptations.

Median and Mode Worksheet

Find the median and mode of the following sets:

1. The number of CDs purchased by students last year:

   2, 3, 3, 4, 8, 8, 7, 6, 6, 6, 5, 4, 3, 6, 7, 8, 8, 9, 3

   median: _____

   mode: _____

2. The amount of times students have ridden the #5 bus in the last month:

   20, 15, 15, 14, 21, 21, 21, 17, 16

   median: _____

   mode: _____

3. The amount of money spent by people in the class on one pair of sneakers this year:

   $95, $85, $79, $75, $59, $29, $29

   median: _____

   mode: _____

4. The months of birthdays in a seventh-grade class:

   9, 9, 6, 6, 6, 5, 5, 3, 3, 3, 8, 8, 7, 7, 7, 7, 2, 1, 12, 11

   median: _____

   mode: _____

5. The number of movies seen last year by a sixth-grade class:

   2, 4, 5, 6, 4, 3,1, 1, 2, 2, 2, 3, 7, 8

   median: _____

   mode: _____

How to Adapt This Lesson for the Inclusive Classroom

For Learning Disabled Students

Review and reteach with a small group of students who are struggling with this concept, using notes you took in class and the worksheet. Strategies such as circling the median and mode with colored pencils will aid students who are visual learners or perceptually impaired.

Students who continue to struggle with the concept of median and mode can use a manipulative. Have students sort and count all candy colors in a bag of colored candies and record the median and mode. This strategy gives students a multisensory example of the concept.

For Resistant Learners and Students with ADD/ADHD

If a student with a behavioral disability is particularly distracted, you can add a kinesthetic modality to learning the concept of median and mode. Working with this small group of students, have them line up by height. It should be easy to see the median and mode this way. Then the students' heights can be measured, recorded on graph paper, and used to calculate the median and mode. The task can be expanded to include different groups of students so the median and mode numbers change. Provide immediate and frequent forms of positive feedback for all students. Use constructive criticism wisely. Rewards such as points or a homework pass may be given for successful participation in this strategy.

For Students with Physical Disabilities

Give these students a small set of hand weights, hackey sacks, or stress balls, and ask them to record how many repetitions or squeezes they can do. Then they can determine the median and mode using these data.

For Gifted Learners

This lesson may be expanded by having gifted students complete an Internet project. Students can go to a weather site online and research the amount of snow and rainfall in their own town or the nearest major city over a period of time. They can chart the information on a piece of poster board and explain what they have learned to the class. They can then lead the class in finding the median and mode with their weather data.

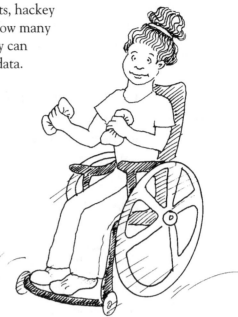

Home/School Connection

Give students the following assignment to complete at home:

> Talk to several extended family members, and find out how much television they watch in a given week. Find the median and mode from these numbers. Record the data, the median, and the mode, and summarize the findings. Bring the results to class to discuss.

How to Evaluate This Lesson

Use a project-centered evaluation. We recommend a review game to assess mastery of this concept. Before the game, write several number sequences on index cards. Students will be asked to find the median and mode of these sequences:

1. Divide the class into four groups.
2. Pass out one reusable plastic mat and one set of erasable markers to each group.
3. Give one index card to each group. Each group will find the median and mode in the number series. Use an egg timer to structure the answering time. The first group to get the correct answer gets a point.
4. The plastic mat will then be passed to the next group member on the right and a different index card given to each group.
5. The rounds continue until all problems are solved.

Assess individual mastery of this concept by observing the strategies of each group member and taking notes on each student during the game.

Activity 3: Circle and Bar Graphs

Purpose: To understand and interpret circle and bar graphs.

Read through the lesson and the adaptations, and make sure you have the supplies you'll need.

For the Main Lesson

chalkboard, overhead projector, computer with presentation software, or interactive whiteboard

unlined paper

index cards

graph paper

colored pencils

compasses

For the Adaptations

colored counters

calculators

Lesson

1. Pass out a piece of unlined paper, a 3 × 5 index card, a compass, a piece of graph paper, and colored pencils to each student.

2. Draw the circle graph shown below on the board, and ask the students to copy this diagram onto their unlined paper using the compass and colored markers.

3. To begin the lesson, you might say: "A circle graph is often used to show the relationship between the variation of parts to a whole and to each other. Here is a diagram of a family budget."

4. Write the data from the circle graph on the board and continue with the lesson: "You can see by the label above the circle graph that the annual monthly income of the family is $4,000. The circle is divided into various sections that represent different percentages of expenditures for the month."

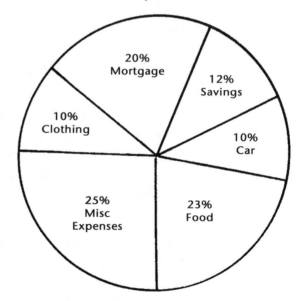

Annual Monthly Income = $4,000

20% Mortgage

12% Savings

10% Clothing

10% Car

25% Misc Expenses

23% Food

Family Budget: Expenditures for One Month

car	10%
savings	12%
clothing	10%
food	23%
mortgage	20%
miscellaneous expenses	25%

5. Explain that you can answer various questions using the data in a circle graph—for example, "How much does the family spend per month on the mortgage payment?"

6. Explain how to answer question 5: "If the total net income is $4,000 a month and the graph tells us that 20 percent of this income would be used for a mortgage payment, you can find out how much is spent on the mortgage by taking 20 percent of 4,000. [Show students how to determine that 20 percent of $4,000 equals $800.] The mortgage payment each month is $800."

7. Ask students to volunteer to formulate another question using the circle graph, and have the rest of the students work the answer to the problem at their seats. Answers can then be reviewed and discussed in class. If the students need additional examples, this exercise can be repeated until the group appears confident and understands how to use the circle graph.

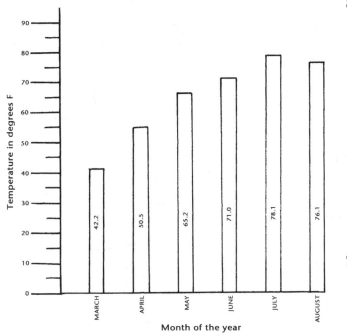

8. Introduce the bar graph in a similar fashion. Draw the bar graph shown here on the board and say something like: "Bar graphs use vertical or horizontal bars to show comparisons between two or more items. Here is a graph that depicts the average monthly temperature for March through August in the Northeast United States. Bar graphs are a good visual way to organize data so that they can be compared quickly and easily."

9. Ask students to formulate questions based on this bar graph. These questions can be written on index cards, collected, and discussed with the class.

Hand out the Circle and Bar Graph Worksheet, and proceed to work with small groups of students on some of the adaptations.

Data Analysis and Probability

Circle and Bar Graph Worksheet

Use the information in the following graphs to answer the questions:

1. Bar graph: **Population of cities found in northern New Jersey in 2006**

   a. Which two cities are closest in population?

   _____

   b. How many more people live in Newark than in Wayne?

   _____

   c. What is the combined population of people who live in Clifton, Garfield, and Paterson?

   _____

   d. Which city has nearly double the population of Glen Rock?

   _____

   e. Within five years, the population of Franklin Lakes is predicted to double. What will the population be at that time?

   _____

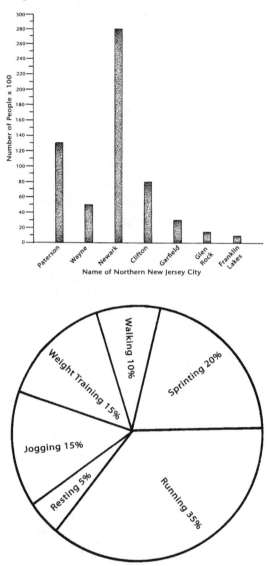

2. Circle graph: **Spring Training Activities for the Track Team**

   The track team is expected to participate in all of these activities in a 2-hour session for the percentage of time shown.

   a. If you were on this track team, how much time would you spend walking at practice?

   _____

   b. Would you spend more time running or jogging during spring training?

   _____

   c. How much combined time would you spend on running and sprinting during each spring training session?

   _____

   d. If you came to practice late one day and missed the weight training segment, how much practice time would you miss?

   _____

How to Adapt This Lesson for the Inclusive Classroom

For Learning Disabled Students

Review and reteach the lesson with a small group of students who are struggling with this concept, using the notes taken in class and the worksheet. Have the students separate a bag of colored counters and create a circle with the counters, grouping them by color. The circle should be able to fit on a piece of paper. This is an easy way to visualize a circle graph. Then students draw lines where each color is and color that piece of the pie.

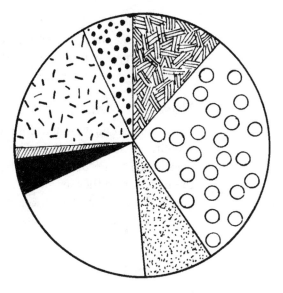

Strategies such as color-coding wedges on circle graphs and using graph paper to draw bars on bar graphs accurately are visual strategies that aid in organizational skills.

A calculator can be used to calculate percentages and check and recheck work.

For students who have difficulties interpreting information presented on a graph, the following mnemonic written on a 3 × 5 index card may be a helpful tool:

USA Strategy

U: Understand and read the title of the graph. Decipher what the graph is attempting to represent.

S: Study the data on the graph. Explain what the graph shows to another person to confirm your thoughts.

A: Answer questions regarding the data. Show all work.

Use the USA strategy to work with students on the worksheet. As they do the problems, have them self-talk by explaining out loud what they are doing in each step.

For Students with Visual Difficulties

This lesson is visual in nature. However, a large-faced calculator and large color-coded models of graphs may be used to give the lesson. Large graphs can be made out of foam board by student and teacher to be used as a manipulative or multisensory aid and saved.

For Gifted Learners

This lesson may be expanded by having gifted learners develop their own circle and bar graphs in a small group. The group should formulate at least three or four questions to analyze graph data and present the graphs and the questions to the class. Students should be encouraged to use the Internet to make their graphs and get ideas. A Web site where students can make their own graphs or get ideas is at the NCES Kids Zone: www.nces .ed.gov/nceskids/graphing/classic.

Data Analysis and Probability

Home/School Connection

Give students the following assignment to complete at home:

> Initiate a family discussion, and decide how much time the family spends together during one week in activities such as household chores, eating together, watching TV, listening to music, visiting, and worship. Make a circle graph depicting the percentage of time spent together for a given week. Bring your graph to class.

How to Evaluate This Lesson

Use a small group presentation. Form students into groups of three based on skill and personalities. Assign each group the task of designing a bar or a circle graph, as well as three questions that are answered by the data presented on their graph. Students may use all of the information they learned in class, as well as the Internet or textbooks, to design their graph. The graph and questions will be handed in collectively for a group grade. The students will be allowed two class sessions to complete this assessment.

Activity 4: Line and Picture Graphs

Purpose: To understand and interpret line and picture graphs.

Read through the lesson and the adaptations, and make sure you have the supplies you'll need.

For the Main Lesson

chalkboard, overhead projector, computer with presentation software, or interactive whiteboard

centimeter squared paper

manila folders

colored pencils

markers

calculators

index cards

For the Adaptations

shoe box

pushpins

1 piece of corrugated cardboard 8 × 8 inches or larger

poster board

1 large bag wrapped colored candies

Lesson

1. Pass out a piece of centimeter squared paper and two 3 × 5 index cards to each student.

2. Draw the line graph shown here on the board, and ask the students to copy this diagram onto their graph paper.

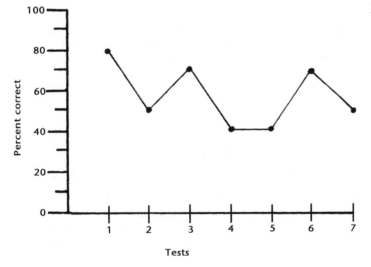

3. To begin the lesson, you might say: "A line graph is used to show changes over distance or time. Here is a line graph that represents Jamie's math test grades for the third marking period. You can see from the graph that we are comparing the scores on tests 1 through 7 for the third marking period. The graph can quickly answer the following questions:"

a. What was Jamie's test score for test 5?

b. What is the difference between Jamie's highest and lowest test score this marking period?

c. How much higher was the score on test 1 than on test 6?

4. Ask students to formulate a question based on the information presented on this line graph, and write it on the index card.

5. Collect all index cards, and ask the questions randomly to the class. Continue until you feel the students have mastered reading this graph.

6. Introduce the picture graph in a similar fashion. Draw the picture graph shown below on the board, and say something like: "Picture graphs are another way to compare data. The pictures are often useful when large amounts of one type of data are present. For example, this picture graph illustrates how many pairs of inline skates were sold in the United States from 2001 to 2006 by a famous toy store chain. Each picture of inline skates on the graph equals 100 pairs of skates. This is the key: Each inline skate equals 100 pairs. The graph can quickly answer the following questions."

1 👟 = 100 pairs   Year

a. How many pairs of inline skates did the toy store sell in 2002?

b. Which two years brought in the most inline skate sales?

c. What year showed the beginning of a decline in inline skate sales?

7. Ask each student to generate one question based on the information presented on the graph and write it on the index card.

8. Collect the index cards, and randomly ask the questions to the class.

Hand out the Line and Picture Graphs Worksheet, and proceed to work with small groups of students on some of the adaptations.

Name: _____   Date: _____

Line and Picture Graphs Worksheet

1. Develop a line graph using the following data on the average amount of milk consumed per person in the United States. Note: You will have two lines of data on the same graph.

Whole	125	105	83	69	55	44	32
Low fat	10	15	25	36	43	52	58
Year	1970	1975	1980	1985	1990	1995	2000

2. Use the information on the line graph to answer the following questions:

   a. In which year did the average person consume the most whole milk? _____

   b. In which year did the consumption of low-fat milk begin to increase? _____

   c. Write a basic statement explaining what you think is the main idea of this graph.

   _____

   _____

3. Develop a picture graph using the following data on the hot wing preference of middle school students in the school cafeteria. Be sure to include a key.

Type of Wings	Mild	Medium	Hot	Fiery	Extra Fiery	Inferno
Number of Students	125	25	180	20	45	10

4. Use the information from the picture graph to answer the following questions:

   a. How many students participated in the cafeteria survey? _____

   b. What is the least favored hot wing preference of middle school students who took this survey?

   _____

   c. What might you conclude about the hot wing preferences of middle school students based on your picture graph?

   _____

   _____

   d. Write a basic statement explaining the main idea of this graph.

   _____

   _____

How to Adapt This Lesson for the Inclusive Classroom

For Learning Disabled Students

Review and reteach the lesson with a small group of students who are struggling with this concept, using the notes taken in class and the worksheet. For students who continue to struggle with the concept of line and picture graphs, you can use a multisensory approach to collecting data to illustrate this concept. Give students a small bag of wrapped candy in assorted colors. Have them sort and count each color and make a picture graph showing the amounts of the different colors of candy.

For students who have difficulties with working memory (remembering information while working through the problem) or auditory processing (processing and using information that they hear) or difficulties interpreting picture and line graphs, writing down the USA Strategy, as presented in Activity 3, on an index card and having students use it as they go through the worksheet may be helpful.

For Students with Visual Impairments

Since these students may struggle to see the intricacies of a line graph, you can use a piece of corrugated cardboard and a set of pushpins to illustrate this concept. Use the pins to mark the data, and draw lines connecting the pins with a thick marker.

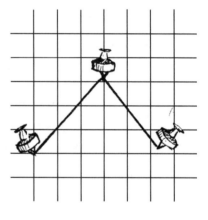

For Gifted Learners

This lesson may be expanded by having gifted learners develop a student survey to collect data for a picture graph. Encourage students to pick a high interest topic, for example, "Five Favorite Football Teams." Students should write team names on a survey with a check box next to each one and deliver them to each homeroom. Surveyed students check off the team they like the most. A ballot box, such as a shoe box with a slit in the top, can be left in each homeroom to collect the data. Students in this group will then develop a picture graph from the data totals and present the graphs on poster board to the class.

Home/School Connection

This project will be presented as the evaluation for this activity at the end of the unit.

> Using Web sites or magazines, such as the Better Business Bureau, *Consumer Reports,* zillions.org, and savvyconsumer.org, research at least three models of a favorite product, such as cars or MP3 players. Record the features and relevant statistics found to support or reject each product choice. Explain which item you feel would make the best choice and why. Make a line and picture graph on poster board comparing specific features of these products. For instance, if the amount of music an MP3 can hold is the most important criterion, graph price along one axis and amount of memory on the other. Bring the finished data and graphs into class. You will be responsible for a five-minute presentation showcasing the products and explaining the graphs. Using props is encouraged!

How to Evaluate This Lesson

Use an individual presentation. Students will present their Home/School Connection project to the class, reviewing various features in their chosen product using line or picture graphs, or both. The presentation, which should last approximately five minutes, will be graded on content, preparation, and delivery.

Activity 5: Investigating Probability

Purpose: To determine and interpret the probability of an event.

Read through the lesson and the adaptations, and make sure you have the supplies you'll need.

For the Main Lesson

chalkboard, overhead projector, computer with presentation software, or interactive whiteboard

lined paper

index cards

For the Adaptations

8 × 11-inch manila folder cut into three strips

black marker

several quarters

colored pencils

Lesson

1. Pass out the lined paper.

2. Write the following definitions on the board, and ask students to copy them on their lined paper:

   Probability. The mathematical likelihood of an occurrence.

   Probability of an event. A mathematical measure that tells the likelihood that an event will occur.

3. To begin the lesson, you might say something like: "Today we will begin studying probability, specifically, the probability of an event. If you are planning for an activity, it is very helpful to know how to interpret probabilities so you can organize effectively.

   "Let's think of probability on a continuum, that is, a scale. Probability is measured on a scale from 0 to 1."

4. Draw the following number line on the board.

$p = 0$	$p = .25$	$p = .50$	$p = .75$	$p = 1$
Will not occur	Probably not	50/50 chance	Probably	Will occur

5. Explain that to find the probability, or likelihood, that a favorable event will occur or have a favorable outcome, divide the number of ways it can occur favorably by the total number of ways that it can occur.

   $$\text{Probability } (p) = \frac{\text{number of favorable outcomes}}{\text{total number of outcomes}}$$

6. Now work a probability-of-an-event problem out on the board.

   Example:

   A small gumball machine holds 30 gumballs:

   10 are red

   6 are green

   12 are yellow

   2 are blue

   If you really wanted to have a green one, what is the mathematical probability of getting the gumball of your choice?

   The total number of outcomes equals how many gumballs are in the gumball machine. Therefore, the total number of outcomes is 30.

   The number of favorable outcomes equals the quantity of your choice present in the machine. There are 6 green gumballs according to the data given. Therefore, the number of favorable choices is 6.

   Now formulate a fraction with the data:

   $$\text{Probability } (p) = \frac{6 \text{ (number of favorable outcomes)}}{30 \text{ (total number of outcomes)}}$$

   Change the fraction to a decimal:

   $$p = \frac{6}{30} = .20$$

   And finish the problem by changing the decimal to a percentage:

   .20 = 20%

   A probability of .20, or 20%, means that you can try for a green gumball 100 times, and out of those 100 times, you can expect (but not guarantee) a green gumball 20 times.

7. If you look at the probability scale on the board, you will see that a 20% likelihood falls closest to the "probably not" section of the scale. So it is not very likely that you would get a green gumball out of this gumball machine.

Hand out the Investigating Probability Worksheet, and proceed to work with small groups of students on some of the adaptations.

Name: _____   Date: _____

Investigating Probability Worksheet

Determine the probability of the following events. (A) Express all probabilities in percents and (B) describe where each event falls on the probability scale (for example, "probably will occur").

1. A jar contains 25 blue marbles and 9 red marbles. What is the probability of drawing a red marble?

   (A)_____

   (B)_____

2. A candy machine designed for a fundraiser holds 200 chocolate, 80 maple, and 1,200 chocolate mint candy bars. Each bar has a special "school spirit" message written on the wrapper. When a dollar bill is inserted into the machine, a random candy bar with a message comes out. What is the probability of getting a maple candy bar?

   (A)_____

   (B)_____

3. A prize jar at the orthodontist includes small plastic treasure chests. There are 40 treasure chests in all. Thirty contain a small sample of flavored toothpaste. Ten contain a free pass to a local movie theater or video arcade. Patients are instructed to pick only one. What are the chances of getting a free pass to the movie theater or video arcade?

   (A)_____

   (B)_____

4. When rolling a standard die, what is the probability of rolling a 2?

   (A)_____

   (B)_____

5. An acoustic piano has 52 white keys. Eight of these are C notes. What is the probability of playing a C if you randomly play a white key?

   (A)_____

   (B)_____

How to Adapt This Lesson for the Inclusive Classroom

For Learning Disabled Students

Review and reteach the lesson with a small group of students who are struggling with this concept, using the notes you have taken in class and the worksheet. A probability scale, similar to the one drawn on the board, can be made using a manila folder strip and a marker. This scale can be taped to the students' desks as a visual representation of the probability of favorable outcomes.

For students who continue to misunderstand this concept, try a multisensory approach. For example, give each student in the group a quarter. Instruct each student to toss the coin 10 times and record the number of times the coin lands heads or tails. Then have students calculate the probability outcome of how often the coin should land on heads and how often it should land on tails. This example can then be expanded by increasing the total number of coin tosses. A calculator can be used to check all work.

To expand the lesson further, give students an example with more possible outcome choices than the coin flip, such as putting different numbers of colored blocks or other objects in a bag and having students pick out one block at a time. What is the probability that they will pull out a red block, a blue block, and so on?

For Resistant Learners and Students with ADD/ADHD

A student with a behavioral disability who is particularly distracted or needs consistent discipline during this lesson may not understand the concepts being presented. If this is the case, the student may participate in the small teaching area or form with other students another small group, depending on the level of the disability. When he or she is working in a separate small group, minimize distractions by clearing away any supplies that aren't needed for the activity. Keep directions simple and to the point. Give only one problem at a time. If the student tends to lose focus after only a few problems on the worksheet, stop immediately, and vary the activity.

Resistant students may enjoy using quarters or candies to illustrate probability calculations, even if they understand how to complete the problems. Multisensory activities can be inserted as a break or bargaining tool when the worksheet is half completed. Provide immediate and positive feedback to students as soon as they return to complete the remaining worksheet problems.

For Gifted Learners

This lesson may be expanded by having gifted learners develop a probability exercise and present it to the class. For example, they could be instructed, "Choose a target percentage, say, 20%. Create a box that will hold a certain number of colored tiles, say, 12. How many blue tiles should you put into the box to give a 20% chance of drawing a blue tile out?"

Home/School Connection

Give students the following activity to do at home. Be sure to give each student a copy of the wheel and spinner patterns on page 185.

Practice finding probabilities by playing the Spinning Wheel of Fortune game with your family; this is a game for two to six players.

Supplies

copy of the wheel and spinner patterns

4 colors of crayons or markers

scissors

1 sheet 8 × 11-inch poster board

white glue

brad

calculator

Directions

1. With the crayons or markers, color each section of the spinning wheel a different color. Cut out the spinning wheel with scissors.

2. Cut off a 1-inch strip of poster board. Put this strip aside.

3. Glue the spinning wheel to the remaining piece of poster board with white glue.

4. Using the spinner pattern, draw the spinner on the 1-inch piece of poster board and cut it out. Attach the spinner to the center of the spinning wheel using the brad.

5. Have each player predict which color will be landed on by developing a probability equation. If the person lands on the predicted color, he or she gets another turn. Otherwise, the player to the right goes next.

6. Keep score of all the correct predictions. The winner of the game is the person who has the most correct predictions. Bring your game into class and share the results.

How to Evaluate This Lesson

Use traditional assessment: a teacher-made quiz to determine students' understanding of the work presented in class, evaluation of class participation, and completion of the Home/School Connection activity.

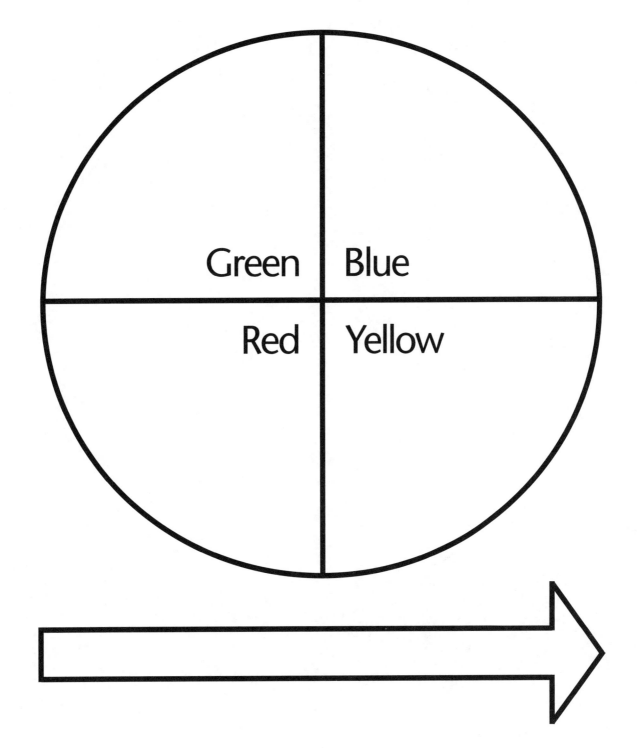

Chapter 8

Problem Solving
and Reasoning

This chapter is designed to aid teachers in presenting information on problem solving and logical reasoning in a multitude of ways in order to address many different learning styles and strengths. Goals are increasing students' ability to use a problem-solving plan as well as strategies such as estimation and logic.

Activity 1: A Problem-Solving Plan

Purpose: To learn an organized and systematic approach to problem solving.

Read through the lesson and the adaptations, and make sure you have the supplies you'll need.

For the Main Lesson

chalkboard, overhead projector, computer with presentation software, or interactive whiteboard

lined paper

For the Adaptations

3 × 5 note cards

colored pencils

large-faced calculators

audiocassette

Lesson

1. Pass out the lined paper.

2. On the board, write the following six-step strategy used to solve word problems, and have students copy it on their paper:

   Step 1. Understand the problem.

   Step 2. Estimate your answer.

   Step 3. Collect the data.

   Step 4. Make an equation.

   Step 5. Solve the equation.

   Step 6. Recheck all work using a calculator.

3. Write the following word problem on the board:

   A total of 500 people went to the bowling alley on Wednesday, 395 on Thursday, and 443 on Friday. About how many people went to the bowling alley over these three days?

4. Show students how to use the six-step strategy to solve the problem:

   Step 1: Understand the problem. Develop a question that tells you what the problem is setting out to solve. In this case, the problem you need to solve is, "How many people went to the bowling alley over these three days?"

   Step 2: Estimate your answer. Once you establish what the problem is looking for, estimate or guess your answer. We know exactly 500 people went on Wednesday. If we rounded to the nearest 10, we could say that approximately 400 people went on Thursday and 440 on Friday, totaling 1,340. This is your estimated answer.

   Step 3: Collect the data. The problem sets out this information:

   > 500: Wednesday
   > 395: Thursday
   > 443: Friday

Step 4: Make an equation. Use the data from step 3:

500 + 395 + 443 =

Step 5: Solve the equation:

500 + 395 + 443 = 1338

Step 6: Recheck your work using a calculator.

5. You may want to complete another problem using this strategy with the group depending on how they seemed to grasp the procedure.

6. Hand out the Problem-Solving Plan Worksheet, and proceed to work with small groups of students on some of the adaptations.

Name: _____   Date: _____

Problem-Solving Plan Worksheet

Solve the following problems using the six-step strategy presented in class.

1. A farm stand sells 12 tomato plants for $8.00. How many plants can you purchase for $22.00?

Step 1: _____

Step 2: _____

Step 3: _____

Step 4: _____

Step 5: _____

Step 6: _____

Problem-Solving Plan Worksheet, Cont'd.

2. A total of 13 buses carried students to a baseball game. There were 48 students on each bus. How many students went to the game?

Step 1: _____

Step 2: _____

Step 3: _____

Step 4: _____

Step 5: _____

Step 6: _____

3. A music company packages 35 CDs in each case for shipping. What is the total number of CDs that can be packed in 175 cases?

Step 1: _____

Step 2: _____

Step 3: _____

Step 4: _____

Step 5: _____

Step 6: _____

How to Adapt This Lesson for the Inclusive Classroom

For Learning Disabled Students

Review and reteach the lesson with a small group of students who are struggling with this concept, using notes taken in class and the worksheet. Each step of the systematic problem-solving plan may be color-coded and placed on a separate 3 × 5 index card with an example so that students may refer to the steps while solving the worksheet problems. A graphic organizer can be used for students who learn 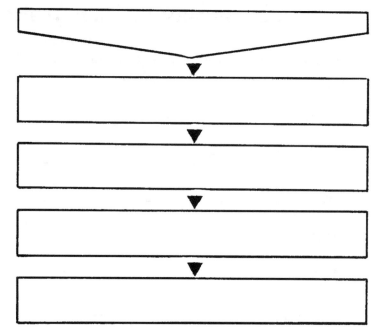 better that way. For example, a piece of paper can be divided into four sections by folding it in half and then in half again. Label each section with one of the steps and write "recheck" in the bottom right corner.

For students who continue to struggle with this process, rereading and paraphrasing word problems may be useful. First, have the students read the word problem aloud. Then ask them to explain what they think the problem is looking to solve. Have the students paraphrase the entire word problem in their own words before using the six-step strategy.

To further aid in understanding, students may be asked to draw a diagram of the word problem. This supplies additional visual representation for students who struggle with short-term memory weaknesses or reading comprehension skills. They can then develop the equation, solve the problem, and recheck using a calculator.

For Students with Physical Disabilities

A large-faced calculator will help students with physical disabilities calculate equations. For students with serious visual or reading disabilities, the teacher can record the six-step problem-solving strategy on an audiocassette. Students listen to the audiocassette while working the problems on the worksheet. They may present their answers orally.

For Gifted Learners

This lesson may be expanded by having gifted learners develop their own jingle or rap song to remember the six-step strategy for problem solving. This song can be presented to the class.

Home/School Connection

Give students the following assignment to complete at home:

> Work with a family member to create a word problem focusing on an everyday occurrence in the family; for example, food preparation, laundry, chores, or bill paying. Write the problem on a 3 × 5 card, and on a separate piece of paper use the six-step strategy to solve the problem. Bring your problem to class.

How to Evaluate This Lesson

Use small group evaluation. Evaluate the Home/School Connection word problems that the students bring to class, and pick twenty that are on an appropriate level for the skills and abilities of the class. Divide students into small groups, and ask them to solve the word problems using the six-step strategy. For students with learning disabilities, you may provide individual help. For example, students who have difficulties with short-term memory or reading comprehension skills may have the problem read to them, and they may be encouraged to draw pictures to be used as a visual aid. For students who process at a slower rate, every other item of the test may be used to assess the mastery of this strategy.

Activity 2: Solving Word Problems Using Estimation

Purpose: To understand how to solve problems through estimation.

Read through the lesson and the adaptations, and make sure you have the supplies you'll need.

For the Main Lesson

chalkboard, overhead projector, computer with presentation software, or interactive whiteboard

lined paper

For the Adaptations

3 × 5 index cards

colored markers

5 rolls of pennies

poker chips

calculators and large-faced calculators

Lesson

1. Pass out a sheet of lined paper to each student.
2. Write the following numbers on the board:

   $2.49 $1.98 $0.69 $0.49 $9.99

3. Write the following word problem on the board, and have students copy it down:

   Zak was going to the Sweet Shop to purchase some candy for his friends. About how much money would Zak need if he spent $2.49, $1.98, $.69, and $.49 on loose candy and $9.99 on a box of fudge?

4. Ask the students to come up with an answer to the problem, drawing their attention to the word *about*.
5. When all the students have finished the problem, start a discussion about the different estimation strategies that they used to solve the problem.
6. Most likely at least one of the students will have used the appropriate estimating technique of rounding up and can describe it to the class. If not, you could say something like this: "If you look at the amount of each item and round it to the nearest dollar or nearest ten cents, you can quickly add up the numbers and find an approximate cost of the candy. Remember that when you're working with money, round the numbers up, or you will be short on cash!" Then show how to work the problem:

   $2.49 = about $3.00 (nearest dollar) or $2.50 (nearest ten cents)

   $1.98 = about $2.00 (nearest dollar)

   $0.69 = about $1.00 (nearest dollar) or $0.70 (nearest ten cents)

   $0.49 = about $1.00 (nearest dollar) or $0.50 (nearest ten cents)

   $9.99 = about $10.00 (nearest dollar)

The total estimated cost to the nearest dollar is $17 ($3 + $2 + $1 + $1 + $10) and to the nearest ten cents it is $15.70 ($2.50 + $2.00 + $0.70 + $0.50 + $10.00). This is the estimated amount of money Zak should bring with him to the candy store.

7. Next, write the following problem on the board, and ask students how they would go about solving it:

Kayla was making 12 pumpkin pies for Thanksgiving. She wanted to know approximately how many cans of pumpkin filling to buy for her project. For each pie, she needs 16 ounces of pumpkin filling. If each can holds 18 ounces, approximately how many cans does Kayla need to buy?

8. Show the class how to break this problem down:

   a. Determine how many ounces of pumpkin filling are needed to make 12 pies. Each pie uses 16 ounces of filling. For 12 pies, multiply the number of ounces needed for 1 pie times the total number of pies:

   16 ounces × 12 pies = 192 ounces for 12 pies

   b. To determine how many cans of pumpkin filling Kayla needs to buy, divide the number of ounces each can holds by the total number of ounces needed for 12 pies. (Students can be encouraged to use the calculator.)

   192 ÷ 18 = 10.6666

   The answer is that 11 cans of pumpkin filling are needed to make 12 pies.

9. Hand out the Solving Word Problems Using Estimation Worksheet, and proceed to work with small groups of students on some of the adaptations.

Name: _____ Date: _____

Solving Word Problems
Using Estimation Worksheet

1. Estimate how many dollars you need to buy each item:

   a a $20.49 sweatshirt _____

   b. a $9.99 tank top _____

   c. an $18.89 handbag _____

   d. a $14.79 belt _____

   e. a $2.99 pair of socks _____

   f. Now estimate how many dollars you need to purchase all of these items. _____

2. Suzanne and Mary Jo went to lunch. Each had a hamburger for $3.59, an order of curly fries for $2.89, and a vanilla milkshake for $2.49. The service was good, so they left a 20 percent tip. Estimate the total cost of the lunch bill.

   _____

196

How to Adapt This Lesson for the Inclusive Classroom

For Learning Disabled Students

Using your notes and strategies learned in class and the worksheet, review and reteach the lesson with a small group of students who are struggling with this concept. Index cards may be used when estimating the cost of items. Place the actual price on one side of an index card. Use a colored marker to write the estimated price on the reverse side. Students may use the calculator to determine the total estimated cost.

For students who continue to have difficulties, multisensory items such as pennies can be useful. Get rolls of pennies from the local bank for students to use to estimate how many pennies are in five wrapped rolls. Have students count the pennies in one roll and multiply that amount times five to estimate the total amount of pennies.

Resistant Learners and Students with ADD/ADHD

A student with a behavioral disability who is particularly distracted or needs consistent discipline during the lesson may be signaling that the concepts presented are too abstract and hard to follow. Using multisensory items may serve to pique interest and keep the learning interactive. If students understand the method but the problems are too easy, make the multisensory problems increasingly difficult.

For Students with Physical Disabilities

Students with visual impairments can use a large-faced calculator.

For Gifted Learners

This lesson may be expanded by having students in this group estimate how many miles, how much gas, and how much money would be needed to plan a road trip for a family of four for one week anywhere in the United States. They can report their findings to the class.

Home/School Connection

Give students the following assignment to complete at home:

> Find a recipe you would like to make with your family. Pick something that has lots of different ingredients. Go to the grocery store, and determine what kind of quantities each item is sold in (for example, in 8-ounce jars, by the dozen, by the pound) and how much they cost. Estimate how many jars, pounds, dozens, and so forth of each item you will need to make your recipe and how much all of the ingredients will cost. Buy the items, and make the recipe with your family. Report to the class how the recipe came out and how your estimating went. Did you have extra of some ingredients? Not enough of anything?

How to Evaluate This Lesson

Evaluate in small groups by playing the game Estimation Mania:

1. Divide students into small groups. Give each group a calculator, lined paper, and pencils. Have each group pick a representative who will give the group's answer.

2. Write a list of prices on the board.

3. Ask the students to estimate the total cost of all of the items written on the board. As soon as each group has an answer, the group's representative should raise his or her hand. The first group with the correct answer receives 1 point.

4. Continue to give students estimating problems using both rounding-up and multiplication strategies.

5. Any students who continue to struggle with this concept may receive additional help after the assessment.

Activity 3: Solving Word Problems Through Logic

Purpose: To understand the thought process needed to solve a problem using logic.
Read through the lesson and the adaptations, and make sure you have the supplies you'll need.

For the Main Lesson
chalkboard, overhead projector, computer with presentation software, or interactive whiteboard
lined paper

For the Adaptations
unlined paper
colored markers
3 × 5 index cards
1 flexible tape measure

Lesson

1. Begin the lesson by saying something like, "So far, we have been learning about how to problem-solve in math using specific strategies, such as a step-by-step formula to break down and organize the information. Today we are going to learn about solving problems using logic."

2. Ask the class to define *logic*. A short discussion may follow. After the discussion, summarize the information provided by the students and provide the following explanation: "A logic problem tests your ability to deduce information from clues provided to reach a specific conclusion. No research is needed. All of the information is provided in the problem. It is especially important to read all of the information, sometimes several times, in order to understand all of the clues provided."

3. Write the following problem on the board, and have students copy it on their lined paper:

   Use the following information to determine the ages of each member of the wood-wind section in the Town Band at the Memorial Day Parade: Kelly, Christi, Tara, Kyle, Dana, and Alexa. The members' ages are 11, 16, 21, 18, 11, and 15.

   a. Christi is six years older than Dana.
   b. Alexa is older than Kyle.
   c. Kelly and Tara are twins.
   d. Dana's Sweet Sixteen party is next week.
   e. Tara is the youngest member.

4. Show the students how to break down the problem to obtain the solution. You might say something like: "First, it is important to read the problem several times in order to process all of the information. Take note of the sentence structure and word choices, because they may serve as clues to the solution. Try solving the problem by creating a chart or graph."

Draw the following chart on the board:

Kelly	Christi	Tara	Kyle	Dana	Alexa
11	21	11	16	15	18

Then say, "Go through each clue carefully. Answer the questions that have the most obvious answers first. For example, the most obvious clue is, 'Tara is the youngest member.' If you look at all the band member ages, you can see that 11 is the smallest number. Therefore, Tara has to be 11 if she is the youngest. However, there are two number 11s in the list. Another clue states that Kelly and Tara are twins. If Tara is 11 and Kelly is her twin, then Kelly must also be 11. Place the number 1 under Tara's and Kelly's names."

Once the more obvious clues are solved, proceed to the more difficult ones. "Let's look at clue d: 'Dana's Sweet Sixteen party is next week.' If Dana's party is next week, then she is not yet 16 so she must be 15. On our list of ages, we have 15. Place the number 15 under Dana's name.

"We now need to find the ages of Christi, Alexa, and Kyle. Now that we know that Dana is 15, we can solve the clue that states that Christi is 6 years older than Dana. If Dana is 15 and Christi is 6 years her senior, that would make Christi 21 years old. Place the number 21 under Christi's name.

"We have deduced all of the band member ages except Kyle and Alexa. The last clue states that Alexa is older than Kyle. With only ages 16 and 18 left in our puzzle, we can deduce that Alexa is 18 and Kyle is 16 years old."

5. Conclude by stating that this is one way to take the clues, break down the information, and use deduction to solve a problem. Brainstorm other strategies with the class that may be helpful when using logic to solve word problems.

6. Hand out the Solving Word Problems Through Logic Worksheet, and proceed to work with small groups of students on some of the adaptations.

Solving Word Problems Through Logic Worksheet

1. Use logic to solve the following problem. Show all of your work. Use a separate piece of paper if necessary.

   Jeannie is having a family reunion this summer. She invited several family members from different parts of the country. Their names are Joseph, Rae, Jackie, Larry, Carol, Lisa, and Bill. Her in-laws, father, aunt, sister, and mother all responded that they could attend. Explain how each of the following people is related to Jeannie:

   a. Joseph is Jeannie's father.
   b. Bill is the brother of Jeannie's husband.
   c. Rae is the sister of Carol.
   d. Jackie is the daughter of Joseph.

   e. Lisa is married to Bill.
   f. Carol is Jackie's mother.
   g. Larry is Lisa's brother.

   Make a chart or grid to explain your answer.

2. Heights and weights were taken by the school nurse in September. The five tallest students in the eighth grade had heights of 6'1", 6.0', 5'11", 5'10", and 5'9". Their names are Sherrye, Paul, Leigh, Ralph, and Austin. Match the heights with the students.
   a. Paul is taller than 6 feet.
   b. Austin is shorter than Paul.
   c. Leigh is the tallest girl.
   d. Ralph is 1 inch shorter than Paul.
   e. Austin is taller than Sherrye and Leigh.

   Make a chart or grid to explain your answer.

201

How to Adapt This Lesson for the Inclusive Classroom

For Learning Disabled Students

Using the notes you have taken in class and the worksheet, review and reteach the lesson with a small group of students who are struggling with this concept. For students who have difficulties knowing how to begin solving a logic puzzle, a mnemonic strategy called the Cross Strategy may serve as a valuable tool.

> ### *The Cross Strategy*
> **C:** Carefully read the entire problem.
> **R:** Reread the problem for understanding.
> **O:** Observe the sentence structure of statements to determine clues.
> **S:** Solve the most obvious clues first.
> **S:** Strategize, making a grid or chart. Draw conclusions based on the data.

Walk students through this step-by-step process using a problem from the worksheet or lesson, or a simpler problem that you create.

Students who continue to struggle with logic problems can be given a premade chart or grid to help them organize the information. You can also help students rewrite each of the problems on the worksheet to include familiar data. This way the students can more readily deduce the outcomes. For example, the family members listed in problem 1 on the worksheet can be substituted with students' actual family members. In problem 2, student heights can be substituted with actual data obtained by using a tape measure to measure all members who are part of this small group.

For students who still find these problems difficult, change the problem to make two clues obvious, and then use the strategies above to draw conclusions.

For Resistant Learners, Students with ADD/ADHD, or Students with Short-Term Memory Weaknesses

Present the information interactively and in small chunks. Write each step of the Cross Strategy mnemonic on a 3 × 5 index card in colored markers. Work through the problem step by step with the student or students in the group. Repeat and restate each step several times to aid in understanding. Do not proceed until the student has mastered each step.

For Gifted Learners

This lesson may be expanded by having gifted learners develop logic word problems. The group may work as a team and present the problems for the class to solve at the end of this activity.

Home/School Connection

Give students the following assignment to complete at home:

> Riddles are often solved using logic. Find at least three riddles that require logic to solve. Copy them down on 3 × 5 index cards, and solve them with your family. Bring the riddles to class for the other students to solve.

How to Evaluate This Lesson

Evaluate using small groups. Group students into pairs; then write a logic problem on the board. Each student pair should solve the problem using class notes or strategies they learned in small groups. They should write down all steps they used to draw conclusions and solve the problem. They should also make a chart or graph that organizes the data.

Answer Key

Chapter Four

Activity 1
Place Value Worksheet

1a.	2	7	4	3	2	6	2
	millions	hundred thousands	ten thousands	thousands	hundreds	tens	ones

1b.	6	2	9	5
	thousands	hundreds	tens	ones

1c.	5	6	7	9	9	4
	hundred thousands	ten thousands	thousands	hundreds	tens	ones

2a. Seven thousand nine hundred eighty-five

2b. One million three hundred forty-two thousand six hundred eighty-one

2c. Eleven thousand five hundred ninety-two

3a. four ones

eight tens

seven hundreds and six tens

three thousands and nine hundreds

4744   four thousands, seven hundreds, four tens, and four ones

3b. one ten, two hundreds, seven thousands, five hundreds, and two tens

six ten thousands, one thousand, eight hundreds, and four ones

69534   six ten thousands, nine thousands, five hundreds, three tens, and four ones

4a. 8742

4b. 3654

Activity 2
Comparing and Ordering
Whole Numbers Worksheet

1a. 34734

1b. 997786

1c. 192

1d. 4435

1e. 27656

1f. 63526

2a. 435 > 347

2b. 995 < 1005

2c. 3465 < 34465

2d. 176 > 169

2e. 187 < 228

2f. 22465 < 22564

3a.
48546	2
48379	1
49284	3

3b. 299482   3

29448   1

298420   2

3c. 38673   3

38592   2

37115   1

4. No; the regular price is only $2.74.

5. Purchasing the tickets three weeks early is the best option. It costs only $117.

Activity 3
Properties of Numbers Worksheet

1. 29; Commutative

2. 168; Associative

3. 0; Zero (Multiplication)

4. 210; Distributive

5. 0; Zero (Multiplication)

6. 12; Associative

7. 24; Distributive

8. 1778; Commutative

Activity 4
Multiples Worksheet

1a. Add 11

1b. 16, 20, 24, 28, 32, 36, 40, 44, 48, 52, 56, 60, 64, 68, 72, 76, 80, 84, 88, 92, 96, 100

Add 4

1c. 24, 30, 36, 42, 48, 54, 60, 66, 72, 78, 84, 90, 96, 102

Add 6

1d. 28, 35, 42, 49, 56, 63, 70, 77, 84, 91, 98, 105

Add 7

1e. 15, 18, 21, 24, 27, 30, 33, 36, 39, 42, 45, 48, 51,54, 57, 60, 63, 66, 69, 72, 75, 78, 81, 84, 87, 90, 93, 96, 99, 102

Add 3

2a. 88, 85, 82, 79, 76, 73, 70, 67, 64, 61, 58, 55, 52, 49, 46, 43, 40, 37, 34, 31, 28, 25, 22, 19, 16, 13, 10, 7, 4, 1

Subtract 3

2b. 55, 40, 25, 10

Subtract 15

2c. 88, 84, 80, 76, 72, 68, 64, 60, 56, 52, 48, 44, 40, 36, 32, 28, 24, 20, 16, 12, 8, 4, 0

Subtract 4

3a. 310 miles

3b. 31 miles on 1 gallon of gas

62 miles on 2 gallons of gas

93 miles on 3 gallons of gas

124 miles on 4 gallons of gas

Multiples Quiz

1. 36, 39, 42, 45, 48, 51, 54, 57, 60, 63, 66, 69, 72, 75, 78, 81, 84, 87, 90, 93, 96, 99, 102

2. 530, 535, 540, 545, 550, 555, 560, 565, 570, 575, 580, 585, 590, 595, 600

3. 92, 90, 88, 86, 84, 82, 80, 78, 76, 74, 72, 70, 68, 66, 64, 62, 60, 58, 56, 54, 52, 50, 48, 46, 44, 42, 40, 38, 36, 34, 32, 30, 28, 26, 24, 22, 20, 18, 16, 14, 12, 10, 8, 6, 4, 2, 0

4. 8, 12, 16, 20, 24, 28, 32, 36, 40, 44, 48, 52, 56, 60, 64, 68, 72, 76, 80, 84, 88, 92, 96, 100

5. 3, 6, 9, 12, 15, 18, 21, 24, 27, 30, 33, 36, 39, 42, 45, 48, 51, 54, 57, 60, 63, 66, 69, 72, 75, 78,81, 84 87, 90, 93, 96, 99, 102

6. 516, 517, 518, 519, 520, 521, 522, 523, 524, 525, 526, 527, 528, 529, 530, 531, 532, 533, 534, 535, 536, 537, 538, 539, 540, 541, 542, 543, 544,545, 546, 547, 548, 549, 550

7. 100, 94, 88, 82, 76, 70, 64, 58, 52, 46, 40, 34, 28, 22, 16, 10, 4

Answers to 8, 9, and 10 will vary. Here are sample responses:

8. To count multiples of five up to 100, you can think of counting nickels up to a dollar. You can also think of it as a pattern with a 0 or 5 in the ones place and numbers zero through nine in the tens place.

9. A multiple of a number is the *product* of that number with any *integer*. We use multiples because they are faster ways of counting.

10. Multiples are used when counting money or telling time.

Activity 5
The Least Common Multiple Worksheet

	Multiples of the First Number	Multiples of the Second Number	LCM
2.	2, 4, 6, 8, 10, 12, 14, 16, 18	9, 18	18
3.	2, 4, 6, 8, 10, 12, 14	7, 14	14
4.	6, 12, 18, 24, 30	10, 20, 30	30
5.	3, 6, 9, 12, 15, 18, 21, 24, 27, 30, 33	11, 22, 33	33
6.	5, 10, 15, 20, 25, 30, 35, 40, 45, 50, 55, 60, 65, 70	14, 28, 42, 56, 70	70
7.	6, 12	12	12
8.	6, 12, 18, 24	8, 16, 24	24
9.	4, 8, 12, 16, 20, 24, 28	7, 14, 21, 28	28

Activity 6
Factoring, Greatest Common Factor, and Prime and Composite Numbers Worksheet

1a. $1 \times 24 = 24$

$2 \times 12 = 24$

$3 \times 8 = 24$

$4 \times 6 = 24$

$6 \times 4 = 24$

$8 \times 3 = 24$

$12 \times 2 = 24$

$24 \times 1 = 24$

1b. $1 \times 64 = 64$

$2 \times 32 = 64$

$4 \times 16 = 34$

$8 \times 8 = 64$

$16 \times 4 = 64$

$32 \times 2 = 64$

$64 \times 1 = 64$

1c. $1 \times 56 = 56$

$2 \times 28 = 56$

$4 \times 14 = 56$

$7 \times 8 = 56$

$8 \times 7 = 56$

$14 \times 4 = 56$

$28 \times 2 = 56$

$56 \times 1 = 56$

1d. $1 \times 48 = 48$

$2 \times 24 = 48$

$3 \times 16 = 48$

$4 \times 12 = 48$

$6 \times 8 = 48$

$8 \times 6 = 48$

$12 \times 4 = 48$

$16 \times 3 = 48$

$24 \times 2 = 48$

$48 \times 1 = 48$

2a. 66

2b. 105

2c. 102

3a. 1

3b. 2

3c. Composite number

3d. Prime factorization

4a. 40

4b. 4

4c. 4

Home/School Connection

1. 35

2. 36

3. 24

Activity 7
Fractions Worksheet

1a. 9/11

1b. 2/9

1c. 2/9

1d. 7/12

1e. 7/8

1f. 4/13

1g. 3/7

1h. 1/3

2a. 12/15

2b. 30/33

2c. 42/45

2d. 93/96

3. a. 3/7 of the students are girls

4. b. 2/3

5a. Answers will vary, for example: 1/4, 2/8, 5/20

5b. Answers will vary, for example: 6/7, 12/14, 30/35

5c. Answers will vary, for example: 8/9, 16/18, 40/45

Fractions Quiz

1a. 2/3

1b. 1/10

1c. 3/7

1d. 3/4

1e. 1/6

1f. 7/11

1g. 11/30

1h. 3/5

2. 76 total pounds of fruit

bananas	19/76 = 1/4
strawberries	14/76 = 7/38
oranges	16/76 = 4/19
grapes	23/76 = 23/76
pineapples	4/76 = 1/19

Activity 8
Percentages and Decimals Lesson

4a. 15/100 = 15% = 0.15

4b. 20/100 = 20% = 0.2

Percentages and Decimals Worksheet

1a. 0.08; 2/25

1b. 0.24; 6/25

1c. 0.47; 47/100

1d. 0.87; 87/100

2a. 56%

2b. 6%

2c. 87.5%

2d. 75%

3a. 86/100; 86%

3b. 5/100; 5%

3c. 34/100; 34%

3d. 67/100; 67%

4. 37/50 = 74/100 = 0.74 = 74%

Percentages and Decimals Quiz

1a. 55%

1b. 80%

1c. 90%

1d. 46%

1e. 43.75%

1f. 31.25%

1g. 83%

1h. 49%

2a. 16%

2b. 33%

2c. 98%

2d. 78%

2e. 64%

2f. 89%

2g. 23%

2h. 55%

3a. 25/100 = 1/4

3b. 56/100 = 14/25

3c. 80/100 = 4/5

3d. 27/100 = 27/100

4. 10/25 = 2/5 = 40%

Chapter 5

Activity 1
The Absolute Value of Integers Lesson

3a. 3

3b. 4

5a. 1.5

5b. 4.5

Absolute Value Worksheet

1. –8

2. (+)16

3. 7

4. 100

5. –$3,000.00

6. 29

7. 36°F

8. $2,000.00

9. –8

10. –6

11a. False

11b. True

11c. True

Activity 2
Adding Integers Worksheet

1. 54 (Rule "a")

2. 0 (Rule "c")

3. –23 (Rule "a")

4. –11 (Rule "b")

5. 0 (Rule "c")

6. 55 (Rule "b")

7. 36 (Rule "a")

8. 34 (Rule "b")

9. 27 (Rule "b")

10. 29 (Rule "a")

11. –5

12. 11

13. –5

14. –5

Activity 3
Subtracting Integers Worksheet

1. 22

2. –49

3. –61

4. –10

5. –32

6. –14

7. –48

8. 0

9. –30

10. 48

11. To subtract an integer, add its opposite.

Home/School Connection

25 + (–15) = 10

10 – (–15) = 25

Subtracting Integers Quiz

1. 10

2. –23

3. –30

4. –27

5. –29

6. –20

7. 0

8. 56

9. 0

10. 79

Activity 4
Multiplying Integers Worksheet

1. –130 (Rule C)

2. –288 (Rule C)

3. 169 (Rule A)

4. –888 (Rule C)

5. –42 (Rule B)

6. 54 (Rule A)

7. –128 (Rule C)

8. 208 (Rule A)

9. –98 (Rule B)

10. –325 (Rule B)

Activity 5
Dividing Integers Worksheet

1. −40 (Rule C)   5. −7 (Rule C)
2. −3 (Rule C)   6. −5 (Rule C)
3. 4 (Rule A)   7. −69 (Rule C)
4. 8 (Rule B)   8. −34 (Rule C)

Activity 6
Plotting Points on a Coordinate Plane Worksheet

1.

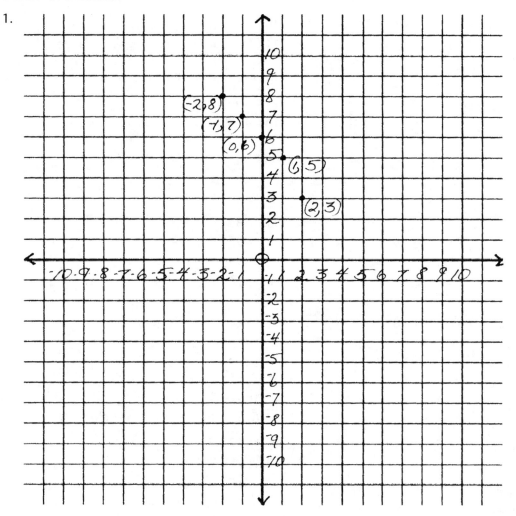

2.

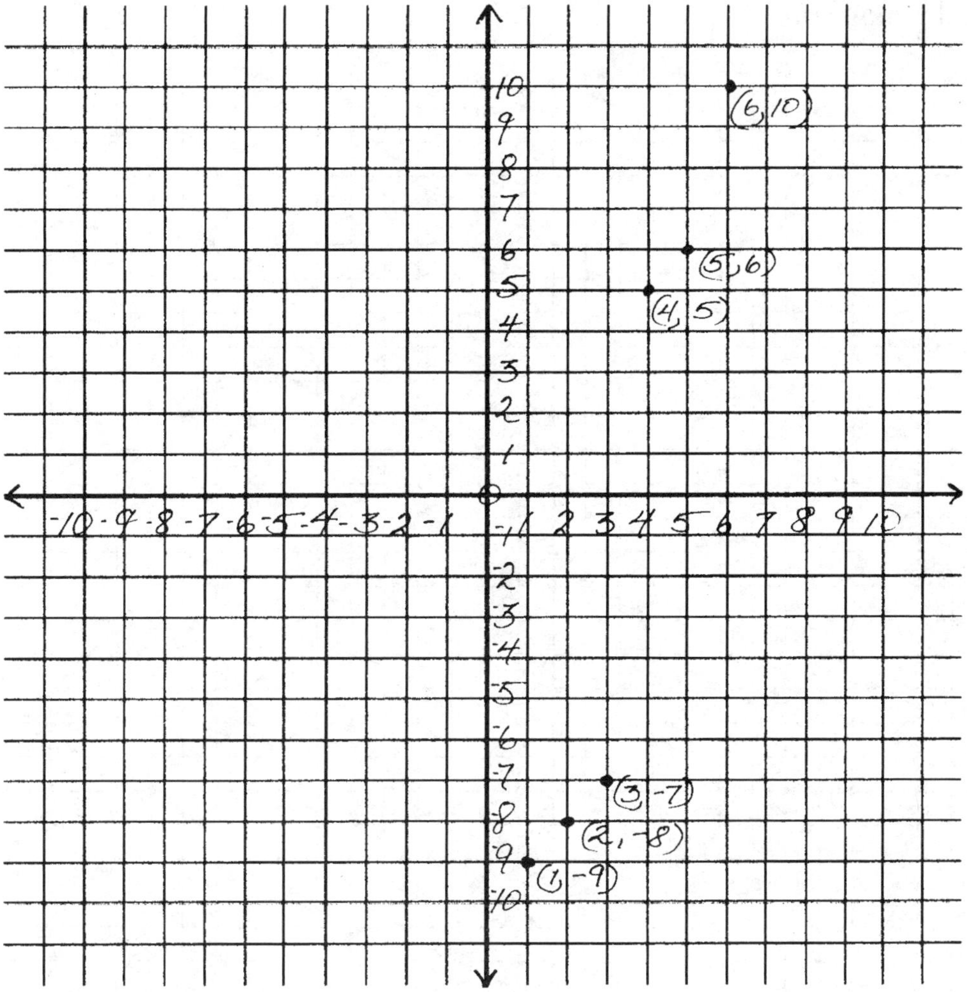
10
9
8
7
6
5
4
3
2
1
-10 -9 -8 -7 -6 -5 -4 -3 -2 -1
-1 1 2 3 4 5 6 7 8 9 10
-2
-3
-4
-5
-6
-7
-8
-9
-10
(6, 10)
(5, 6)
(4, 5)
(3, -7)
(2, -8)
(1, -9)

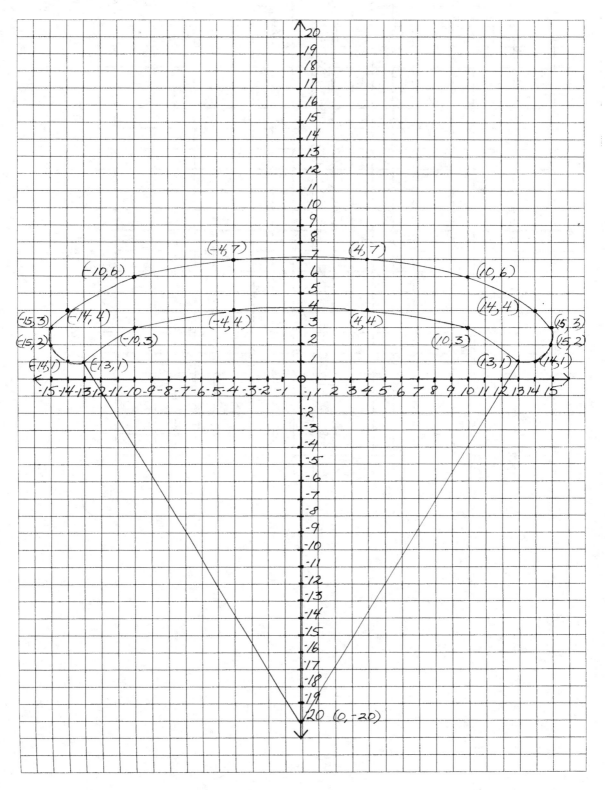

Activity 7
Integers and Exponents Worksheet

1a. -4^6
1b. -6^4
1c. -5^5
1d. -2^6
2a. $-6,561$
2b. -972
2c. -343
2d. 29

Activity 8
Rates Worksheet

1. 5 in/hr; 10 in/2 hrs; 15 in/3 hrs; 20 in/4 hrs; 25 in/5 hrs
2. $15/day
3. 2.25 min (2 min, 15 sec)/question
4. 2,000 Cal/day; 4,000 Cal/2 days; 10,000 Cal/5 days; 56,000 Cal/month (month = 4 weeks)
5. 50 words/min; 250 words/5 min; 20 min to type the term paper

Chapter 6

Activity 1
Lines and Angles Worksheet

1. 90°
2. any angle less than 90°
3. any two angles whose degree values add to 180°
4. any angle greater than 90°
5. any two angles whose degree values add to 90°
6. any set of two intersecting lines
7. any set of lines that will never intersect
8. lines that intersect and for a 90°angle

Activity 2
Basic Geometric Shapes Worksheet

1. One pair of opposite sides is parallel
2. All side equal, all right angles
3. Two pairs of equal parallel sides
4. Three sides
5. Opposite sides parallel
6. Six sides
7. Eight sides
8. Five sides

Attachment: drawings on graph paper of the shapes listed on the worksheet

Activity 3
Triangles and the Pythagorean Theorem Worksheet

1a. Scalene
1b. Right
1c. Equilateral
1d. Isosceles
1e. Scalene
1f. Equilateral
2a. $c = 8.6023252$
2b. $c = 12.806248$
2c. $c = 6.4031242$

Activity 4
Area and Perimeter of Quadrilaterals and Triangles Worksheet

1a. 16 ft
1b. 11 ft
1c. 144 ft
1d. 66 ft
2a. 84 ft^2
2b. 77 ft^2
2c. 54 ft^2
3a. 400 ft^2
3b. 60 ft^2
3c. 96 ft^2
3d. 132 ft^2

Activity 5
Properties of Circles Worksheet

1a. The distance from the edge of a circle to its center. The radius, or r, is always one-half the diameter of the circle.

1b. A line segment that passes through the center of the circle and has both endpoints on the circle. The diameter cuts the circle exactly in half. Equal to the radius times two.

1c. The distance around a circle. Equal to pi times the diameter.

1d. The amount of space inside a circle. Equal to pi times the radius times the radius, or πr^2.

2a. 28.26 ft

2b. 5 ft

2c. 113.04 ft^2

2d. 12 ft

Activity 6
Polyhedrons Worksheet

1a. A polyhedron in which the base is a polygon and all other faces are triangles

1b. A polyhedron with two congruent and parallel faces

1c. A polygon that makes a side of a polyhedron

1d. A three-dimensional figure that has polygons for faces

1e. A line segment where the faces of a polyhedron meet

1f. On a polyhedron, a point where three or more edges meet

2. Rectangular prism: 6 faces, 8 vertices, 12 edges

   Triangular pyramid: 4 faces, 4 vertices, 6 edges

   Octahedron: 8 faces, 6 vertices, 12 edges

   Triangular prism: 5 faces, 6 vertices, 9 edges

   Cube: 6 faces, 8 vertices, 12 edges

Activity 7
Surface Areas of Prisms Worksheet

a. 600 in^2

b. 2,160 in^2

c. 24 ft^2

d. 460 cm^2

e. 396 in^2

Chapter 7

Activity 1
Finding the Mean Worksheet

1. $3.71

2. 240.4444 pages

3. 63.25°F

4. 25.5 mph

5. 71.16666 seconds

For Gifted Learners

1. 2000

2. 1350

Activity 2
Median and Mode Worksheet

1. Median: 6, mode: 3, 6, 8

2a. Median: 17, mode: 21

3a. Median: $75, mode: $29

4a. Median: 6.5, mode: 7

5a. Median: 3, mode: 2

Activity 3
Circle and Bar Graph Worksheet

1a. Glen Rock and Franklin Lakes

1b. 23,000

1c. 24,000

1d. Garfield

1e. 2,000

2a. 12 minutes

2b. Running

2c. 1 hour, 6 minutes (66 minutes)

2d. 18 minutes

Activity 4
Line and Picture Graphs Lesson

3a. 40

3b. 40 points

3c. 10 points

6a. 2200

6b. 2001 and 2002

6c. 2003

Line and Picture Graphs Worksheet

1. Graphs will vary.

2a. 1970

2b. 1970

2c. This graph shows that people are switching from drinking whole milk to drinking low-fat milk.

3.

Type of Wings

Mild	Medium	Hot	Fiery	Extra Fiery	Inferno

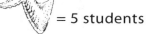 = 5 students

4a. 405

4b. Inferno

4c. They like the mild and hot wings the best.

4d. This graph displays students' preferences for particular kinds of hot wings.

Activity 5
Investigating Probability Worksheet

1. (A) 26.470588%; (B) probably not

2. (A) 5.4054%; (B) probably not

3. (A) 25%; (B) probably not

4. (A) 16.6666%; (B) probably not

5. (A) 15.384615%; (B) probably not

Chapter 8

Activity 1
Problem-Solving Plan Worksheet

1. Step 1: How many plants can you purchase for $22.00?

    Step 2: 30 plants (or any other well-supported answer)

    Step 3: 12 plants cost $8.00

    Step 4: $22.00 ÷ $8.00 = 2.75

    Step 5: 2.75 × 12 = 33

    Step 6: 33 plants

2. Step 1: How many students went to the game?

    Step 2: 600 students (or any other well-supported answer)

    Step 3: 48 students on each bus; 13 buses

    Step 4: 48 × 13 = 624

    Step 5: 624 students

    Step 6: 624 students

3. Step 1: How many CDs are there in total?

    Step 2: 6,000 CDs (or any other well-supported answer)

    Step 3: 35 CDs in each case; 175 cases

    Step 4: 32 × 175 = 5,600

    Step 5: 5,600 CDs

    Step 6: 5,600 CDs

Activity 2
Solving Word Problems Using Estimation Worksheet

1a. $21.00 or $20.50

1b. $10.00

1c. $19.00 or $18.90

1d. $15.00 or $14.80

1e. $3.00

1f. $68.00 or $67.20

2. $12.00 or $10.80

Activity 3
Solving Word Problems Through Logic Worksheet

1a. Joseph is Jeannie's father.

1b. Bill is Jeannie's brother-in-law.

1c. Rae is Jeannie's aunt.

1d. Jackie is Jeannie's sister.

1e. Lisa is Jeannie's sister-in-law.

1f. Carol is Jeannie's mother.

1g. Larry is Jeannie's brother-in-law.

2a. Paul is 6'1".

2b. Sherrye is 5'9".

2c. Leigh is 5'10".

2d. Ralph is 6'0".

2e. Austin is 5'11".

National Council of Teachers of Mathematics Standards Chart

National Council of Teachers of Mathematics, *Principles and Standards for School Mathematics* (Reston, Va.: National Council of Teachers of Mathematics, 2000).

Chapter 4	Standards	Standard Reference
Activity 1: Place Value	Understand numbers, ways of representing numbers, relationships among numbers, and number systems	NM-NUM 3-5.1
Activity 2: Whole Numbers	Understand numbers, ways of representing numbers, relationships among numbers, and number systems	NM-NUM 3-5.1 NM-NUM 6-8.1
Activity 3: Properties of Numbers	Understand meanings of and how they relate to one another	NM-NUM 3-5.2 NM-NUM 6-8.2
Activity 4: Multiples	Understand numbers, ways of representing numbers, relationships among numbers, and number systems	NM-NUM 6-8.1
	Compute fluently and make reasonable estimations	NM-NUM 3-5.3 NM-NUM 6-8.3
Activity 5: Least Common Multiple	Understand numbers, ways or representing numbers, and number systems	NM-NUM.3-5.1 NM-NUM 6-8.1
	Compute fluently and make reasonable estimations	NM-NUM 3-5.3
Activity 6: Prime/Composite Numbers	Understand numbers, ways of representing numbers, relationships among numbers, and number systems	NM-NUM 6-8.1
	Understand meanings of operations and how they relate to one another	NM-NUM 3-5.2

Chapter 4 (cont'd)	Standards	Standard Reference
Activity 7: Fractions	Compute fluently and make reasonable estimations	NM-NUM 3-5.3
	Understand meanings of operations and how they relate to one another	NM-NUM 6-8.2
Activity 8: Percentages/Decimals	Understand numbers, ways of representing numbers, and number systems	NM-NUM 3-5.1 NM-NUM 6-8.1
	Understand meanings of operations and how they relate to one another	NM-NUM 6-8.2

Chapter 5	Standards	Standard Reference
Activity 1: Absolute Value of Integers	Represent and analyze mathematical situations and structures using algebraic symbols	NM-ALG 3-5.2
	Understand patterns, relations, and functions	NM-ALG 6-8.1
Activity 2: Adding Integers	Represent and analyze mathematical situations and structures using algebraic symbols	NM-ALG 3-5.2 NM-ALG 6-8.2
	Use mathematical models to represent and understand quantitative relationships	NM-ALG 3-5.3 NM-ALG 6-8.3
Activity 3: Subtracting Integers	Represent and analyze mathematical situations and structures using algebraic symbols	NM-ALG 3-5.2 NM-ALG 6-8.2
	Use mathematical models to represent and understand quantitative relationships	NM-ALG 6-8.3
Activity 4: Multiplying Integers	Represent and analyze mathematical situations and structures using algebraic symbols	NM-ALG 3-5.2 NM-ALG 6-8.2
	Use mathematical models to represent and understand quantitative relationships	NM-ALG 6-8.3
Activity 5: Dividing Integers	Represent and analyze mathematical situations and structures using algebraic symbols	NM-ALG 3-5.2 NM-ALG 6-8.2
	Use mathematical models to represent and understand quantitative relationships	NM-ALG 6-8.3

Chapter 5 (cont'd)	Standards	Standard Reference
Activity 6: Plotting Points	Use mathematical models to represent and understand quantitative relationships	NM-ALG 3-5.3 NM-ALG 6-8.3
	Represent and analyze mathematical situations and structures using algebraic symbols	NM-ALG 6-8.2
	Analyze change in various contexts	NM-ALG 6-8.4
Activity 7: Integers and Exponents	Use mathematical models to represent and understand quantitative relationships	NM-ALG 3-5.3
	Represent and analyze mathematical situations and structures using algebraic symbols	NM-ALG 3-5.2 NM-ALG 6-8.2

Chapter 6	Standards	Standard Reference
Activity 1: Types of Lines and Angles	Understand measurable attributes of objects and the units, systems, and processes of measurement	NM-MEA 3-5.1 NM-MEA 6-8.1
	Analyze characteristics and properties of two- and three-dimensional geometric shapes and develop mathematical arguments about geometric relationships	NM-GEO 3-5.1 NM-GEO 6-8.1
Activity 2: Shapes	Analyze characteristics and properties of two- and three-dimensional geometric shapes and develop mathematical arguments about geometric relationships	NM-GEO 3-5.1 NM GEO 6-8.1
	Use visualization, spatial reasoning, and geometric modeling to solve problems	NM-GEO 3-5.4 NM-GEO 6-8.4
Activity 3: Triangles	Apply appropriate techniques, tools, and formulas to determine measurements	NM-MEA 6-8.2
	Analyze characteristics and properties of two- and three-dimensional geometric shapes and develop mathematical arguments about geometric relationships	NM-GEO 6-8.1 NM-GEO 3-5.2
	Specify locations and describe spatial relationships using coordinate geometry and other representational systems	NM-GEO 6-8.2

Chapter 6 (cont'd)	Standards	Standard Reference
Activity 4: Area and Perimeter	Analyze characteristics and properties of two- and three-dimensional geometric shapes and develop mathematical arguments about geometric relationships	NM-GEO 6-8.2
	Use visualization, spatial reasoning, and geometric modeling to solve problems	NM-GEO 3-5.4 NM-GEO 6-8.4
Activity 5: Circles	Apply appropriate techniques, tools, and formulas to determine measurements	NM-MEA 6-8.2
	Use visualization, spatial reasoning, and geometric modeling to solve problems	NM-GEO 3-5.4 NM-GEO 6-8.4
Activity 6: Polyhedrons	Apply transformations and use symmetry to analyze mathematical situations	NM-GEO 3-5.3 NM-GEO 6-8.3
	Use visualization, spatial reasoning, and geometric modeling to solve problems	NM-GEO 3-5.4 NM-GEO 6-8.4
Activity 7: Surface Area of Prisms	Apply appropriate techniques, tools, and formulas to determine measurements	NM-MEA 3-5.2 NM-MEA 6-8.2
	Use visualization, spatial reasoning, and geometric modeling to solve problems	NM-GEO 3-5.4 NM-GEO 6-8.4

Chapter 7	Standards	Standard Reference
Activity 1: The Mean	Select and use appropriate statistical methods to analyze data	NM-DATA 3-5.2 NM-DATA 6-8.2
Activity 2: The Median and Mode	Formulate questions that can be addressed with data; and collect, organize, and display relevant data to answer	NM-DATA 3-5.1 NM-DATA 6-8.1
	Select and use appropriate statistical methods to analyze data	NM-DATA 3-5.2
Activity 3: Circle and Bar Graphs	Select and use appropriate statistical methods to analyze data	NM-DATA 3-5.2 NM-DATA 6-8.2
	Develop and evaluate inferences and predictions that are based on data	NM-DATA 3-5.3 NM-DATA 6-8.3

Chapter 7 (cont'd)	Standards	Standard Reference
Activity 4: Line and Picture Graphs	Select and use appropriate statistical methods to analyze data	NM-DATA 3-5.2 NM-DATA 6-8.2
	Develop and evaluate inferences and predictions that are based on data	NM-DATA 3-5.3 NM-DATA 6-8.3
Activity 5: Investigating Probability	Understand and apply basic concepts of probability	NM-DATA 3-5.4 NM-DATA 6-8.4

Chapter 8	Standards	Standard Reference
Activity 1: A Problem-Solving Plan	Build new mathematical knowledge through problem solving	NM-PROB.PK 12.1
	Apply and adapt a variety of appropriate strategies to solve problems	NM-PROB.PK 12.3
	Monitor and reflect on the process of mathematical problem solving	NM-PROB.PK 12.4
	Organize and consolidate their mathematical thinking through communication	NM-PROB.COMM.PK 12.1
	Communicate their mathematical thinking coherently and clearly to peers, teachers, and others	NM-PROB.COMM.PK 12.2
Activity 2: Solving Word Problems Using Estimation	Solve problems that arise in mathematics and in other contexts	NM-PROB.PK 12.2
	Apply and adapt a variety of appropriate strategies to solve problems	NM-PROB.PK 12.3
	Compute fluently and make reasonable estimates	NM-NUM 3-5.3 NM-NUM 6-8.3
Activity 3: Solving Word Problems Through Logic	Recognize reasoning and proof as fundamental aspects of mathematics	NM-PROB.REA.PK 12.1
	Select and use various types of reasoning and methods of proof	NM-PROB.REA.PK 12.4
	Solve problems that arise in mathematics and in other contexts	NM-PROB.PK 12.2

Glossary

Absolute value: the distance of a number from zero.

Acute angle: an angle that measures less than 90 degrees.

Adjacent angles: two angles that share a vertex or a side but don't overlap.

Angle: an angle formed by the intersection of two rays with a common endpoint.

Area: the number of square units that covers a shape or figure.

Associative Property of Addition and Multiplication: the order in which the numbers in a problem are grouped does not affect the answer.

Circle: the set of points in a plane that are a fixed distance from a given point, called the center.

Commutative Property of Addition and Multiplication: when you switch the order of two numbers being added or multiplied, the answer does not change.

Complementary angle: two angles whose measures add up to 90 degrees.

Composite number: a positive integer that is not prime.

Coordinate plane: the plane determined by a horizontal number line, called the x-axis, and a vertical number line, called the y-axis, intersecting at a point called the origin. Each point in the coordinate plane can be specified by an ordered pair of numbers.

Decimal: another way to write a percentage.

Denominator: the bottom part of a fraction.

Distributive property: Multiplication may be distributed over addition. If you have a problem where you're adding two numbers and multiplying the sum by a third number, you could instead "distribute" the third number and multiply it by both of the numbers you want to add, then add the products.

Edge: a line segment where the faces of the polyhedron meet.

Exponent: a number that indicates the operation of repeated multiplication.

Face: a polygon that makes up one of the sides of a polyhedron.

Fraction: part of a whole.

General education teachers: those who specialize in one area of the curriculum, such as English, history, math, reading, or science.

Greatest common factor: the largest number that divides two or more numbers evenly.

Guidance counselors: those who work as a liaison with teachers, students, parents, administration, and Child Study Team.

Integers: the set of numbers containing zero, the natural numbers, and all the negatives of the natural numbers.

Kite: two pairs of consecutive equal sides.

Learning disabilities teacher/consultant or educational therapist (LDT/C) or educational diagnostician): those who complete psychoeducational testing to determine students' academic strengths and weaknesses and develop remedial modifications to aid in therapeutically teaching students with disabilities.

Least common multiple: the smallest nonzero number that is a multiple of two or more numbers.

Mean: the mathematical average obtained from a set of numbers.

Median: the middle number in a set of numbers when the numbers are arranged in numerical order.

Mode: the number that occurs most often in a set.

Multiple: the product of a number and any other whole number. Zero is a multiple of every number.

Numerator: the top part of a fraction.

Obtuse angle: an angle that measures more than 90 degrees but less than 180 degrees.

Occupational therapists: those who evaluate and provide therapies to strengthen fine motor and organizational skills.

Octagon: an eight-sided polygon.

Oval: an egg-shaped or elliptical form or figure.

Parallel lines: lines in a plane that are the same distance apart at all points.

Parallelogram: a quadrilateral with opposite sides parallel.

Paraprofessionals: those who assist teachers in implementing group and individual lesson plans.

Pentagon: a five-sided polygon.

Percent: how many per hundred or a fraction whose denominator is 100.

Perimeter: the sum of the lengths of the sides of a polygon.

Perpendicular lines: lines that intersect, forming right angles.

Personal aides: those who act as personal assistants to students in the classroom.

Physical therapists: those who evaluate and provide therapies to strengthen gross motor skills.

Polygon: a closed plane figure made up of several line segments that are joined together.

Polyhedron: a solid (three-dimensional) figure that has polygons as its faces.

Prime number: a number whose only factors are itself and 1.

Prism: a polyhedron with two congruent (the same) and parallel faces.

Probability: the mathematical likelihood of an occurrence.

Pyramid: a polyhedron in which the base is a polygon and the other faces are triangles. The triangles share a common vertex.

Ray: part of a line, with one endpoint, and extending to infinity in one direction.

Rectangle: a quadrilateral with four 90-degree angles.

Rhombus: a quadrilateral with opposite sides parallel.

School nurse: a nurse who completes vision and hearing screenings, checks attendance, and offers specific nursing services to special and general education students.

School psychologist: the person who assesses learning levels, academic levels, and emotional or behavior concerns of students who are referred to the Child Study Team.

School social worker: the person who obtains student and family background information and determines if this is having an impact on the student's educational performance.

Special education teachers: those who teach skills and strategies for remediation purposes and are in part responsible for implementing the educational modifications designated in Individual Education Programs.

Speech and language therapists: those who determine if a student's articulation and language abilities have a negative impact on learning success in school.

Square: a quadrilateral with four equal sides and four 90-degree angles.

Supplementary angles: two angles whose measures add up to 180 degrees.

Surface area: area of a three-dimensional figure, the sum of the areas of all the faces.

Trapezium: a quadrilateral that has exactly two sides parallel.

Triangle: a three-sided polygon.

Vertex: on a polyhedron, a point where three or more edges meet.

Vertical angles: two angles formed by intersecting lines.

Zero property of addition: adding zero to a number leaves the number unchanged.

Zero property of multiplication: multiplying any number by zero gives you zero.

Additional Resources

Association for Supervision and Curriculum Development, http://www.ascd.org. ASCD as a community of educators advocates sound policies and shares best practices to achieve the success of each learner.

Council for Exceptional Children, http://cec.sped.org. The CEC is dedicated to improving educational outcomes for individuals with exceptionalities, students with disabilities, and the gifted. It advocates for appropriate governmental policies, sets professional standards, and provides professional development.

Learning Disabilities Association of America, http://www.ldaamerica.org. LDA is a nonprofit volunteer organization advocating for individuals with learning disabilities. The membership, which consists of individuals with learning disabilities, family members, and concerned professionals, advocates for school-age students with learning disabilities and for adults.

LDonline, www.ldonline.org. LD OnLine provides information on learning disabilities, learning disorders, and differences. Parents and teachers of learning disabled children will find guidance on attention deficit disorder, attention deficit–hyperactivity disorder, dyslexia, dysgraphia, dyscalculia, dysnomia, reading difficulties, speech, and related disorders.

Math for America, http://www.mathforamerica.org. Math for America was founded to improve the quality of mathematics education in public schools by working with teachers, school administrators, and parents.

National Association for Gifted Children, http://www.nagc.org/. NAGC uses its resources to train teachers, support parents, and educate administrators and policymakers on how to develop and support gifted children.

National Center for Learning Disabilities, http://www.ncld.org/. NCLD provides information to parents, professionals, and individuals with learning disabilities; promotes research and programs; and advocates for policies to strengthen educational rights and opportunities.

National Council of Teachers of Mathematics, http://www.nctm.org. NCTM provides vision, leadership, and professional development to support teachers in ensuring mathematics learning of the highest quality for all students.

Bibliography

Batshaw, M., and Perret, Y. M. *Children with Disabilities: A Medical Primer*. Baltimore, Md.: Brookes Publishing, 1996.

Brooks, R., and Goldstein, S. *The Power of Resilience*. New York: McGraw-Hill, 2004.

Brown, T. *Attention Deficit Disorder: The Unfocused Mind in Children and Adults*. New Haven, Conn.: Yale University Press Health and Wellness, 2005.

Bulgren, J. A., and Schumaker, J. B. *The Paired Associates Strategy: Learning Strategies Curriculum*. Lawrence: University of Kansas Center for Research on Learning, 1996.

Campbell, L., Campbell, B., and Dickinson, D. *Teaching and Learning Through Multiple Intelligences*. (3rd ed.) Needham Heights, Mass.: Allyn & Bacon, 2003.

Canter, L., and Canter, M. *Succeeding with Difficult Students: New Strategies for Reaching Your Most Challenging Students*. Santa Monica, Calif.: Canter and Associates, 1993.

D'Amico, J., and Drummond, K. *The Math Chef: Over 60 Math Activities and Recipes for Kids*. Hoboken, N.J.: Wiley, 1996.

Gardner, H. *Multiple Intelligences: The Theory in Practice*. New York: Basic Books, 1993.

Krulik, S., Rudnik, J., and Milov, E. *Teaching Mathematics in Middle School: A Practical Guide*. Needham Heights, Mass.: Allyn and Bacon, 2002.

Larson, R., Boswell, L., Stiff, L., and Kanold, T. *Passport to Mathematics-Book 2*. Evanston Ill.: McDougal Littell, 2001.

Lerner, J., and Kline, F. *Learning Disabilities and Related Disorders: Characteristics and Teaching Strategies*. Boston: Houghton Mifflin, 2005.

Neuschwander, C. *Sir Cumference and the Dragon of Pi*. Watertown, Mass.: Charlesbridge, 2002.

————. *Sir Cumference and the First Round Table*. Watertown, Mass.: Charlesbridge, 2002.

Yanoff, J. C. *The Classroom Teacher's Inclusion Handbook*. Chicago: Arthur Coyle Press, 2000.

Index

Individual Education Program (IEP), 4
Individuals with Disabilities Act (IDEA), 11
Integer Dance Explosion (I-Dance Explosion), 85
Integer Hold'Em, 99–100
Integers, 224
Integers and exponents activity, 107–110; answers, 213; evaluation, 110; for gifted learners, 110; home/school connection, 110; for learning disabled students, 110; worksheet, 109
Intelligence characteristics, identifying, 22
Internet, monitoring, 14
Interpersonal intelligence, 21
Intervention and Referral Services Committee (IRS), 8, 10, 12
Intrapersonal intelligence, 21
Investigating probability activity, 180–185; answers, 216; evaluation, 184; for gifted learners, 183; and home/school connection, 183–184; for learning disabled students, 183; for resistant learners and students with ADD/ADHD, 183; worksheet, 182
"Investigation of a Chocolate Chip Cookie" activity, 52
IRS. *See* Intervention and Referral Services Committee

K

Kinesthetic learners, 19, 20
Kite, 224

L

LDonline, 227
Learning Disabilities Association of America, 227
Learning disabilities teacher/consultant or educational therapist (LDT/C), 224; as member of Child Study Team, 6
Learning disables students, 23
Learning styles: assessing, 19–20; fitting teaching strategies to, 21; and learning strengths, 20–21
Least common multiple, 224
Least common multiple activity, 55–58; answers, 207; evaluation, 58; for gifted learners, 58; home/school connection, 58; for learning disabled students, 57; for resistant learners and students with ADD/ADHD, 58; for students with physical disabilities, 58; worksheet, 56
Least restrictive environment (LRE), 11
Lerner, J., r
Line and picture graphs activity, 175–179; answers, 213, 215–216; evaluation, 179; for gifted learners, 178; and home/school connection, 178; for learning disabled students, 178; for students with visual impairments, 178; worksheet, 177

Logic/math intelligence, 20
LRE. *See* Least restrictive environment

M

Math for America, 227
Mean, 224
Median, 224
Mode, 224
Modeling: educational behavior, 14
Movie watching, guiding, 14
Multiple, 224
Multiple intelligences: and learning strengths, 20–21
Multiples activity, 49–54; for all learners, 52; answers, 206; evaluation, 52; for gifted learners, 52; home/school connection, 52; for learning disabled students and students with visual impairments, 52; quiz, 54; worksheet, 51
Multiplying integers activity, 92–95; for all learners, 94–95; answers, 209; evaluation, 95; for gifted learners, 94; home/school connection, 95; for learning disabled students, 94; for physically disabled students, 95; for resistant learners and students with ADD/ADHD or with short term memory and organizational difficulties disabilities, 94; worksheet, 93
Musical/rhythmic intelligence, 21

N

Name That Shape, 132
National Association for Gifted Children, 227
National Center for Learning Disabilities, 227
National Council of Teachers of Mathematics, 227; Standards Chart, 217–221
NCES Kids Zone, 173
Neuschwander, C., 142
Numbers and operations, 33–74; and comparing and ordering whole numbers, 40–43; and factoring, greatest common factor, and prime and composite numbers, 59–64; and fractions, 64–69; and least common multiple, 55–58; and multiples, 49–54; and percentages and decimals, 70–74; and place value, 34–39; and properties of numbers, 44–48
Numbers, properties of (lesson), 44–48; for gifted learners, 47–48; handout, 45; home/school connection, 48; for learning disabled or visually impaired students or resistant learners, 47; worksheet, 46
Numerator, 224

O

Obtuse angle, 119, 224
Occupational therapist, 224; as member of Child Study Group, 8

W

Whole numbers, comparing and ordering, 40–43; for gifted learners, 43; and home/school connection, 43; for learning disabled students, 42; for resistant learners and students with ADD/ADHD, 42–43; for students with physical disabilities, 42; worksheet, 41

Y

Young teens, reading with, 13

Z

Zero property of addition, 225
Zero property of multiplication, 225
zillions.org, 178